VOLUME 32

GRIFFON-POWERED
SPITFIRES

BY KEV DARLING

specialtypress
PUBLISHERS AND WHOLESALERS

COPYRIGHT © 2001 KEV DARLING

Published by
Specialty Press Publishers and Wholesalers
11605 Kost Dam Road
North Branch, MN 55056
United States of America
(651) 583-3239

Distributed in the UK and Europe by
Midland Publishing
4 Watling Drive
Hinckley
LE10 3EY
England

ISBN 1-58007-045-0

All rights reserved. No part of this book may be reproduced or transmitted in any form or by any means, electronic or mechanical including photocopying, recording, or by any information storage and retrieval system, without permission from the Publisher in writing.

Material contained in this book is intended for historical and entertainment value only, and is not to be construed as usable for aircraft or component restoration, maintenance, or use.

Printed in China

Front Cover: *Seen on the ground, Spitfire FR.XIV MV293 reveals the location of the wing walkways, the structure of which was strengthened to reduce damage to the upper surfaces. (Nick Challoner)*
Back Cover (Left Top): *Turning toward the photographer at the beginning of a simulated TacR flyby is Supermarine Spitfire MV268 wearing the personal markings of air ace "Johnny" Johnson. (Danny Jacquemin)*
Back Cover (Right Top): *After the first 25 PR.19s were built, the rest were equipped with a pressure cabin to allow reconnaissance flights at a greater height. (Eric B Morgan Collection)*
Back Cover (Lower): *Seen from a slightly different angle, this view reveals even more of the detail underneath the Spitfire PR.19 including some of the panel lines. Note that the radiator flaps are fully retracted when the aircraft is manoeuvring at speed. (Dave Stewart)*
Title Page: *This underside view of MV293 reveals the location of the underwing radiator fairings, the undercarriage bays, and the tail wheel doors. (Nick Challoner)*

TABLE OF CONTENTS

GRIFFON-POWERED SPITFIRES

	PREFACE 4	
	INTRODUCTION AND ACKNOWLEDGMENTS	
CHAPTER 1	**PAST AND FUTURE** 5	
	THE DEVELOPMENT OF THE SPITFIRE MK.XII	
CHAPTER 2	**SPITFIRES FOR THE MANY** 15	
	THE SPITFIRE F.XIV AND F.XVIII	
CHAPTER 3	**SPITFIRE IN THE BLUE** 31	
	THE SPITFIRE PR.19	
CHAPTER 4	**"SUPER SPITFIRE"** 45	
	THE SPITFIRE F.21, F.22, AND F.24	
COLOR SECTION	**COMBAT COLOURS** 65	
	OF THE SPITFIRE AND SEAFIRE	
CHAPTER 5	**SPITFIRES AT SEA** 73	
	THE GRIFFON SEAFIRES	
CHAPTER 6	**FINAL FLING** 93	
	THE SPITEFUL AND THE SEAFANG	
APPENDIX A	**SPITFIRE ALPHABET** 102	
	ACRONYMS AND ABBREVIATIONS	
APPENDIX B	**SIGNIFICANT DATES** 103	
	KEY DATES IN THE HISTORY OF THE GRIFFON-POWERED SPITFIRE	

PREFACE

INTRODUCTION AND ACKNOWLEDGMENTS

In the eyes of many people the Griffon-powered Spitfires and their derivatives were the epitome of grace. In contrast to the more rounded contours of the earlier Merlin Spitfires the greater angularity of the later types exuded a sense of greater power. Added to the structural changes was the ability to carry an increased variety of weapons at faster speeds and longer distances.

All, however, was not that successful as the last manifestation of the design would prove. The Spiteful and Seafang undertook their maiden flights just as the jet age was getting into full swing and for all their laminar flow wings and other refinements they could not compete on level terms as a succession of jet fighters entered service with the Royal Air Force. With their demise came the end of the Spitfire line, although the wing technology was to reappear again on the jet-powered Supermarine Attacker for the Fleet Air Arm.

This slim volume attempts to tell the story of the Griffon-powered aircraft from the first tentative steps of the Mk.XII to full-blown production aircraft in the shape of the FR.18 and the F.24. In order that the story should appear complete, the seagoing versions of the Spitfire, the Griffon Seafires, are also included. Within these covers are the in-depth details of the fighter versions plus the photo reconnaissance variants and their usage by the strangely named THUM (Temperature and Humidity) flight.
Overseas use of the Griffon Spitfire is also covered, thus images from as far apart as Thailand to Egypt appear. The adventures of the late marque Seafires of the Fleet Air Arm in Korea are also covered where they performed their task admirably, sometimes against great odds.

The appearance of the jet fighter saw the Spitfire being replaced by such types as the Gloster Meteor and the De Havilland Vampire. They were to remain in service with the Royal Auxiliary Air Force until its sudden disbandment on 10 March 1957. In the service of the Fleet Air Arm the Seafire and other piston-powered aircraft lasted slightly longer until they too were replaced by jet aircraft, although in this instance they came from the same builder, Supermarine.

This then is the story of the second generation of the Supermarine Spitfire in words, pictures, and technical diagrams from a slightly different perspective. For helping me create this work I would like to thank the following: Peter Russell Smith for allowing me access to his extensive photo collection yet again; the doyen of Spitfire historians, Eric B Morgan for access to his collection of Spitfire material and for his inimitable assistance; and Chris Michell of Airframe Assemblies based on the Isle of Wight for taking time out to photograph a series of disassembled aircraft for me. Others worthy of mention include Damien Burke, Nick Challoner, Danny Jacquemin, Dave Stewart, and Sander Wittenaar.

Yet again I make mention of Dennis R Jenkins for his design layout and of Dave Arnold and all at Specialty Press for their assistance and long-distance support.

Kev Darling
Vale of Glamorgan, Wales
February 2001

Roaring through the murk past the camera is Spitfire FR.XIV, MV268, with its radiator flaps fully deployed. The peculiar aspect of the light brings out some of the airframe panel lines. (Danny Jacquemin)

Past and Future

The Development of the Spitfire Mk.XII

To better understand the need for the Griffon-powered Spitfire it is necessary to review the development of the previous Merlin-engined variants of the aircraft and their relationship in combat to their counterparts in the Luftwaffe, in particular the Messerschmidt Me-109E and the Focke-Wolf FW-190.

In the mid-1930s the Royal Air Force (RAF) was primarily equipped with biplanes in almost all the major combat and transport roles and constrained by government-imposed financial restrictions. In contrast the German Luftwaffe was already operating monoplanes in the fighter, bomber, and transport roles and subjecting them to combat evaluation in the Spanish Civil War. As this war progressed each of the aircraft types under consideration was developed in light of experience gained, thus armaments, engines, and aerodynamics came in for close scrutiny. Meanwhile, in total contrast, the RAF was using its biplanes for such arduous tasks as policing Iraq and other countries in the Middle East.

Although this period in world history appears as one of appeasement, there were those in Britain that had seen the signs of impending war in Europe. One of those visionaries was R J Mitchell, the chief designer at Supermarine Aircraft. During the period 1925 to 1931 the company had designed and built a series of racing seaplanes designated the S.4, S.5, and S.6 respectively. All had exhibited two primary features which were to fit the biggest engine possible into the smallest, most streamlined airframe possible.

With these aircraft the company and a dedicated RAF piloting team finally won the World Airspeed Record and the Schneider Trophy with a top speed of 407 mph. However, a small production run of eight racing sea-

The main opponent for the Spitfire during the Battle of Britain and other air-to-air engagements was frequently the Messerschmidt Me-109. This is the preserved "E" version "Black 6." (Big Bird Aviation Collection)

The appearance of the Spitfire Mk.Vc was a much needed upgrade to the Spitfire genre. This clipped wing Mk.Vc featured an upgraded powerplant plus Hispano cannons as standard.
(Dave Stewart)

planes does not make for a great profit margin. A financial lifeline from the Vickers Engineering Group was able to save the company and its expertise from an early demise.

At the same time the Air Ministry issued a specification for a new monoplane fighter to replace the biplane Gloster Gauntlet and other similar fighter aircraft. This resulted in the appearance of the crank-winged Type 224 as the Supermarine contender. However, flight trials soon revealed that the aircraft was a poor performer and the whole concept was revamped, although it did feature some revolutionary ideas such as inset wing radiators. Eventually, after much design work and refinement, the Supermarine Type 300 prototype was rolled out and the Spitfire was born.

The first flight of K5054 translated into a production order for 310 Spitfire Mk.Is which began to enter squadron service with the No. 19 Sqdn on 4 August 1938. It entered alongside examples of the Hawker Hurricane which were on the strength of other units. Although production was erratic, where fuselages were being built quicker than the more complex wings, deliveries to frontline units were eventually to even out to a consistent level. In light of the events taking place in Europe this was a good thing.

To buy time for a hasty rearmament the British Prime Minister, Neville Chamberlain, had gone to Munich to create "peace in our time." However, this period of grace ended on 3 September 1939 when war was declared. The subsequent events surrounding the British Expeditionary Force and the later Battle of Britain are not for discussion here, but may be covered in a later volume.

The basic Spitfire that entered RAF service was an eight-gun Merlin-powered aircraft equal in most respects to its Luftwaffe counterpart, the Messerschmidt Me-109E. Modifications to the basic Spitfire had seen the upgraded Merlin II and III fitted to the aircraft as well as an enlarged propeller boss covering the pitch change mechanism which replaced

Following on from the earlier Messerschmidt was the FW-190. Radial power, a neat airframe, and good armament made the aircraft a real handful for allied pilots. This is the rare two-seat version of this aircraft.
(Big Bird Aviation Collection)

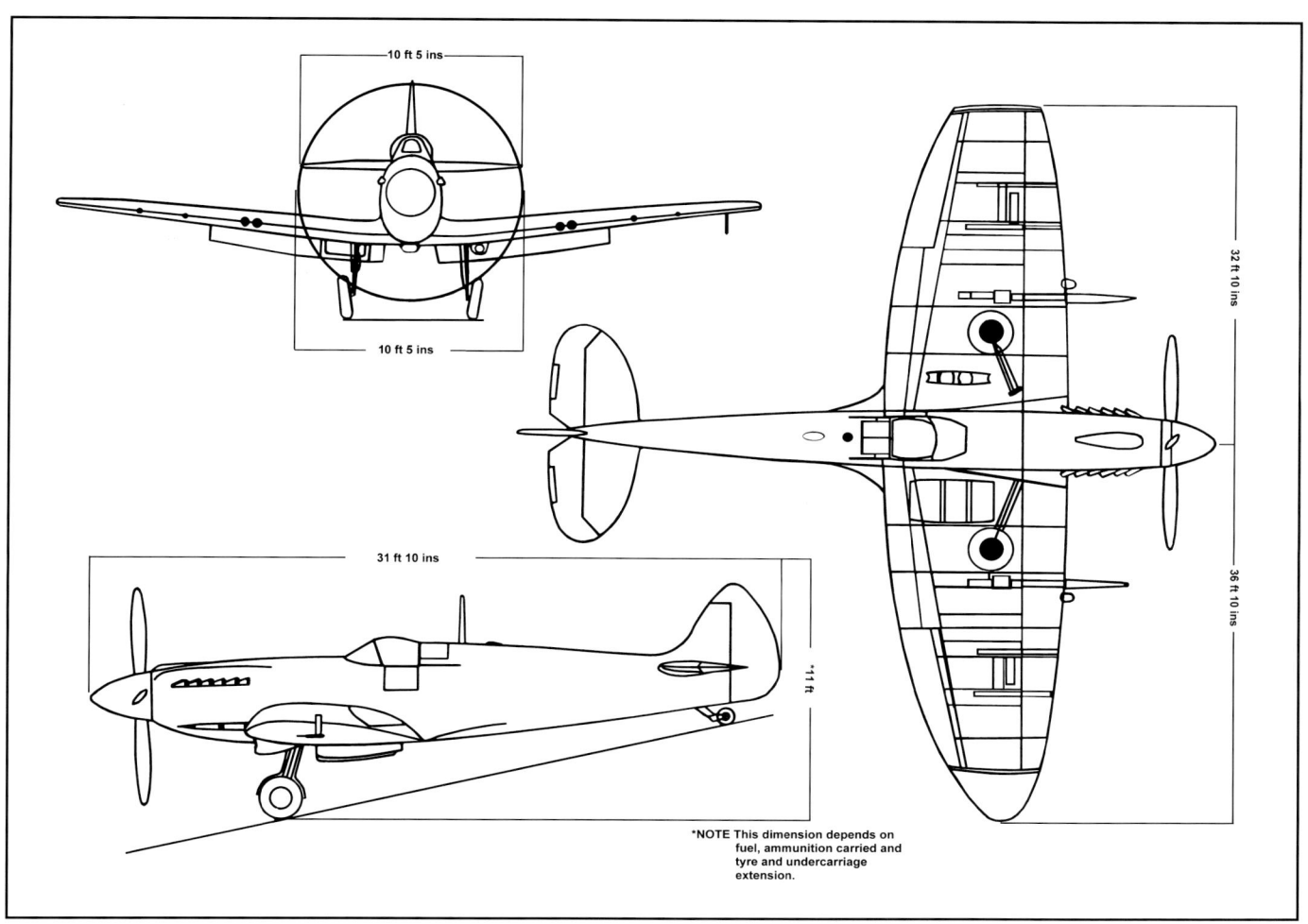

This general arrangement diagram shows the version of the Spitfire XII that was based on the Spitfire Mk.Vc. Both the earlier pointed and cut off wingtips are shown although the latter were standard. The second batch of the type was based on the Mk.VIII airframe and had retractable tail wheels. (Big Bird Aviation Collection)

the earlier wooden fixed pitch assembly. Armament was also altered in some airframes when 20mm Hispano cannons replaced the earlier eight gun Browning .303 armament. This resulted in the machine-gun equipped aircraft becoming designated the Mk.IA whilst the others became the Mk.IBs.

A further extension of the Spitfire's capabilities appeared when a reconnaissance version was developed. Stripped of armament, much armour plate, and with all excess weight removed, these aircraft, initially painted pink, carried out daring high-speed runs across targets in occupied Europe. They paved the way for a multi-function version of the fighter at a later date.

However, before such functionality could be achieved, the Spitfire would develop through a variety of marques to meet evolving challenges. The next version of the Spitfire would be the Mk.II which would feature as its primary change the upgraded Merlin XII powerplant. Deliveries to the RAF began in August 1940 just in time to take part in the Battle of Britain. In common with the earlier Mk.I the new version had two wing types which resulted in the Mk.IIA with machine guns and the Mk.IIB with twin cannons and four machine guns.

The appearance of the Spitfire V was a defining moment in the development of the genre. The aircraft was virtually a standard airframe with the major difference being the strengthening of the engine bulkhead and bearers to take advantage of the more powerful Rolls Royce (R-R) Merlin 45. The first production examples were the eight gun Mk.VA. However, manufacture changed to the Mk.VB after some 94 examples had been built. This version, as with all "B" designated aircraft, had an armament of two His-

Seen by many as the starting point for the Spitfire, the Supermarine S.6 exemplified the concept of a large engine fitted to a slender aerodynamic airframe. To celebrate the life of designer R J Mitchell, this aircraft now resides in the Southampton Hall of Aviation. (C P Russell Smith Collection)

pano cannons and four .303 Browning machine guns. Entry into service began in February 1941 with almost all operational units fully equipped by the end of the year.

A further development of the Spitfire resulted in the Mk.IX which was desperately needed to combat the German Focke-Wolf FW-190 that had proven more than capable of outflying the earlier Spitfires. The primary changes were the installation of the Merlin 61 engine coupled to a four-bladed propeller, both of which gave the airframe improved handling and speed above 38,000 feet.

As with other versions of the Spitfire, the Mk.IX was optimised for a variety of roles including low- and high-level interception plus, of course, the inevitable reconnaissance role. A further variation on the theme was the Mk.XVI where the major airframe changes were the replacement of the high-back fuselage with a bubble canopy and cut-down rear fuselage for increased all-around vision and the installation of American-built Packard Merlin powerplants.

The first major revision in the construction of the Spitfire came about with the appearance of the Mk.VIII. It featured a radically strengthened airframe, retractable tail wheel, and leading edge fuel tanks in the wings. The powerplant was still the Rolls Royce Merlin coupled to a four-bladed propeller. It was reckoned by many pilots to be the best-handling version of the Merlin-powered genre.

Development of the Griffon engine had begun at Rolls Royce just prior to the outbreak of war as the designers of the previous 27-litre Merlin had realised that the engine parameters of that engine could be pushed only so far. By drawing on the design of the "R" class engines as fitted to the racing seaplanes and by extending the overall dimensions marginally, the engine was increased in size to 36.7 litres and thus the Griffon was born.

As the new engine was only slightly larger (in that the frontal area had increased from 7.5 square feet to 7.9 square feet) it was obvious that the Spitfire would make a good recipient. Following this thread the head of the design team at Supermarine, Joe Smith, submitted a design proposal to the Air Ministry as Specification No. 466 in October 1939. This resulted in a pair of airframes being ordered as the Spitfire Mk.IV.

The first Spitfire Mk.IV, DP845, made its maiden flight from the Supermarine airfield at Worthy Down on 27 November 1941 piloted by Chief Test Pilot Jeffrey Quill. The powerplant was a single stage supercharged Griffon, RG 2SM, IIB driving a four-bladed propeller.

Handling was described as superb especially at low level where the extra power would later be much appreciated, although great care was needed with throttle operation during takeoff. Only one small problem would mar the praise of these early engines and that was one of reliability.

Flight testing also revealed another bugbear that would follow the Griffon-engined Spitfires throughout their development. This was the problem of longitudinal stability to which would be coupled the aircraft's behaviour during power changes which resulted in greater trim changes. A series of armament options was tried on this aircraft, these being a six cannon wing, four 20mm cannons, and the standard two cannons and four machine guns. Not long after this the Spitfire Type 366 was redesignated the Mk.XX as the previous notation was required for a reconnaissance version. This first of the Griffon Spitfires was changed yet again, this time to the Mk.XII.

Although the Merlin-powered versions of the Spitfire were developing nicely, the rest of Fighter Command's future fighter policy was in total chaos. Hopes had been pinned on the Hawker Tornado powered by the R-R Vulture engine. However, this aircraft was in deep trouble due to compressibility problems causing structural failures whilst the engine had the embarrassing habit of stopping at the most inopportune moments.

Realising that the problems with the Vulture could never be resolved in a reasonable time scale, the development of the aircraft using this powerplant was stopped. Happily, both types involved, the Avro Manchester bomber and the Tornado, were to achieve greater fame later as the Merlin-powered Lancaster and the Napier Sabre-powered Typhoon ground attack fighter. To partially alleviate the situation, Fighter Command and the concerned Ministries decided to press on with developing the Spitfire powered by a single-stage Griffon although this solution was recognised as not ideal from the outset.

The production version of the Spitfire Mk.XII featured a two cannon, four machine gun "B" wing whilst the retractable tail wheel was borrowed from the contemporary Mk.VIII. The wing was very similar to the Mk.V complete with semi-circular oil cooler and a slightly enlarged box-shaped radiator. This, however, did not completely reduce the engine overheating problem that afflicted the Mk.XII throughout its service life.

Testing at low level revealed a fighter that could outperform the Hawker Typhoon and a captured Fw-190. The revelation of the new aircraft was carried out in front of a selection of dignitaries in the form of a race, not very scientific, but entertaining nevertheless. Although the betting was on the German fighter to win, the result was that the Spitfire came first followed by the Typhoon and lastly by the Focke-Wulf.

Production of the Spitfire Mk.XII as the Type 366 was handled by Supermarine and consisted of the basic Mk.V fuselage with modifications plus strengthening of the engine bearers to take the Griffon powerplant. This was to change in the main production batch to that of the Spitfire Mk.VIII which was a far stronger and adaptable airframe. One change

Spitfire IIA, P7530, served with No. 266 Sqdn and No. 603 Sqdn before transferring to other duties. Compared with the Griffon-engined versions of the same aircraft, the roundness of the fin and rudder, plus the slightly shortened nose associated with the Merlin, can clearly be seen. (Big Bird Aviation Collection)

The progenitor of the Spitfire PR.19 was the much-used PR.XI, exemplified here by the pink-finished PL965. Although the Griffon-powered PR.19 was an advance on the earlier Merlin-powered aircraft, its appearance did not spell the end for the earlier types as the PR.19 took over most of the high-altitude duties. (Dave Stewart)

from DP845 that featured in the production version was clipping of the wings which improved aileron roll rate at low level.

Testing of the aircraft was undertaken at the Aircraft and Armament Experimental Establishment (A&AEE) Boscombe Down, using DP845 during the period September through October 1942. Initially the aircraft was flown with a narrow chord rudder reminiscent of that fitted to the earlier Spitfire Mk.IB. This empennage was later replaced by that from an Mk.V complete with the fixed tail wheel from that marque.

Following on from its time at Boscombe Down the Spitfire was transferred to the Air Fighting

The Spitfire Mk.IX was seen as a temporary stopgap before the more definitive Mk.VIII became available in quantity. However, this was not the case as many versions of this versatile variant were produced. (Big Bird Aviation Collection)

Development Unit (AFDU) which put it through its paces as a combat aircraft. The AFDU's report was very enthusiastic, especially concerning the Spitfire's performance at low to medium altitudes where it outperformed all the fighters on the then-current inventory of the RAF. The report did, however, mention the longitudinal problem, stating that in certain parts of the flight envelope the rudder was ineffective and required constant trimming.

Retained as a test bed, DP845 also flew with another early version of the Griffon, the Mk.IV. Trials were carried out with a variety of propellers including a five-bladed unit although this revealed an increase in the drag coefficient which led to a reduction in top speed. The more powerful Griffon had a greater tendency to torque the Spitfire and the smaller rudder was replaced by a broader chord item similar to that fitted to the later Mk.IX. This helped to compensate for the type's tendency to swing on takeoff, although the aircraft was still very sensitive to engine throttle adjustments which required constant trimming.

Even these changes were not enough to ensure that the aircraft was always a stable gun platform. To confuse the pilots even more the engine rotated in the opposite direction to that of the Merlin, thus inducing a severe swing to the right. To assist the pilots in coping with this change to the operating procedure, the tyre pressures were increased as was the inflation pressure in the port undercarriage leg.

The engine itself exhibited many changes from the earlier Merlin powerplant. One of the main differences was that of starting procedure. For the Merlin this required a 12-volt power source and some fuel system priming whilst the Griffon used the Coffman cartridge starter. This device contained five shotgun-like cartridges although a rough start from one of these early engines could sometimes result in a greater consumption than that contained within the breech especially if the pilot treated it like a Merlin and primed the fuel system.

Another change encountered with the Griffon was a reduction in the number of magnetos to one which were housed under a skin blister above the engine. The fuel system also underwent revision producing some interesting behaviour in early squadron service as it exhibited a tendency to cut out whether the aircraft was experiencing positive or negative "G" forces. Eventually, after extensive test flights and experimentation, changes to the carburation solved this problem.

To provide the Griffon with its extra boost, it was fitted with a two-speed, single-stage supercharger which

The Spitfire LF.16 was a development of the Mk.IX which featured a cut down rear fuselage, a bubble canopy, and a Packard-built Merlin engine. (Big Bird Aviation Collection)

Spitfire F.XII, MB878, was one of the batch built using Mk.VIII fuselages. This aircraft never saw squadron service with the Royal Air Force, it was retained for testing purposes instead. Here it is in flight trials with the centreline 500-pound bomb and mount. (Eric B Morgan Collection)

took its drive from the front of the engine, the shaft for which ran through the oil sump. This ensured that the aircraft achieved its best performance at approximately 18,000 feet even though the Mk.XII actually spent most of its operating life at 1,800 feet where its top speed of 325 mph gave it a positive advantage.

The first production Spitfire Mk.XII, EN222, was rolled out in November 1942. In contrast to earlier versions the fuselage was flush riveted thus reducing airframe drag. A total of 100 production Spitfires of this marque were manufactured and equipped Nos. 41 and 91 Sqdns in February and June 1943 respectively. Both units were much travelled in their task, remaining at some places for only a period of months. In July 1944 No. 41 Sqdn was based at Lympne, Kent, when it traded in its aircraft for the later Mk.XIV following the lead of No. 91 Sqdn which had re-equipped in February.

This is a close up of the Mk. III bomb mount and 500-lbs. bomb undergoing testing on MB878. (Eric B Morgan Collection)

The frontline service career of the Mk.XII ended with the No. 595 Sqdn with flights based at various locations in West Wales where the aircraft patrolled the Irish Sea. This last stint lasted from December 1944 until July 1945 when the squadron disbanded.

Not all airframes entered squadron service, as a handful found themselves involved in trials work. One was EN223 which spent some time at AFDU, Duxford, for tactical trials whilst EN224 became involved in trials aimed at reducing the torque-induced swing of the aircraft on takeoff. Another two airframes, EN226 and EN227, spent some time being evaluated by the Admiralty for possible Fleet Air Arm (FAA) use. For this purpose they were fitted with an "A" frame arrestor hook borrowed from a Seafire Mk.III, standard full-span wingtips, and an auxiliary rear oil tank. Trials and evaluation flights were carried out at Arbroath by the FAA Service Trials Unit where many practise deck landings took place. Although the Mk.XII was not accepted for FAA use, in its standard RAF form, it led to the development of the Seafire XV.

Technical specifications of the Spitfire Mk.XII were a span of 32 feet 7 inches with an area of 231 square feet whilst the fuselage length was 30 feet 9 inches. The powerplants fitted to the aircraft included the Griffon III and the Griffon IV although this featured in only 24 aircraft. All had a Rotol four-bladed propeller installed with a diameter of 10 feet 5 inches. Basic fuel contents were 85 gallons which gave an endurance of 35 minutes if the Spitfire were flown at full bore. The later batch of aircraft, serialled in the MB range, were capable of carrying a 30-gallon overload tank. This in itself could cause some problems during release. On at least two occasions the teleflex release change-over cable successfully released the tank, but shut off the primary fuel system thus causing the aircraft to crash due to fuel starvation. Another minor problem that frequently annoyed the pilots was the delay in the new fuel gauging delivering system contents which could be embarrassing.

A standard armament was installed in the wings of the Mk.XII. This comprised the Universal "B" wing setup of two 20mm Hispano cannons with 60 rounds per gun plus four .303 Browning machine guns with 350 rounds per gun. The aircraft was also cleared to carry the standard 250-pound or 500-pound General Purpose (GP) bomb on the centreline for "hit and run" missions over Europe, although these were not extensive.

Performance was measured over a range of heights. At a height of 2,000 feet a maximum of 355 mph was possible increasing to 392 mph at 24,000 feet. The service ceiling of the Mk.XII was set at 37,350 feet and

The predecessor to the Spitfire Mk. XII was the Mk.IV that was powered by an Rolls Royce Griffon engine. This view shows DP845 carrying a mock-up installation of the six Hispano cannon installation. (Eric B Morgan Collection)

maximum range was given as 493 miles. Basic weights were 5,580 pounds tare with a maximum overload of 7,400 pounds. As well as the standard armament, the Spitfire Mk.XII had a combat cine gun installed in the port wing. In total contrast to the first versions of the Spitfire it positively bristled with communications equipment as it featured the TR9D, TR1133, R3002, and A2171AB radio systems.

In service the Spitfire Mk.XII was intended for low-level fighter sweeps over occupied Europe where it could perform most efficiently. However, the pilots of the Luftwaffe were markedly reluctant to engage in this kind of combat, preferring to stay at higher altitudes where they were in combat with the Spitfire HF.IX. They were also allocated a task within the Air Defence of Great Britain where their intended role was to shoot down the low-level hit-and-run raiders dispatched by the Luftwaffe. Flying the FW-190, the Luftwaffe managed to evade the defending forces, thus the two squadrons were in desperate need of improved ground radar warning to enable them to intercept these random raiders. However, this was not always available and successes were few and far between.

It took the advent of the V.1 flying bomb attacks against targets in southeast England for the Mk.XII to come into its own. Its superior speed and handling allowed the fighter to intercept and shoot down a great number of these weapons before they struck their targets. Some other trials were carried out in September 1943 on the Mk.XII when at least one was fitted with a centre-line pylon and a 500-pound bomb so that the RAF could conduct its own hit and run raids over Europe. This idea would eventually result in both squadrons together becoming a wing at West Hampnett where they undertook strike fighter raids over Normandy up to altitudes of 15,000 feet.

The Spitfire Mk.XII was not an outstanding success overall, although it eventually found its niche in the air defence organisation. However, it did pave the way for the subsequent versions that followed and proved that the Griffon engine was a viable powerplant worthy of further development. Its tenure in the ranks of the RAF was fairly short-lived as it was replaced in frontline squadrons during late 1944 by other versions of the Griffon Spitfire before being declared totally redundant for flying purposes in February 1946. A handful did see some extra service as ground instructional airframes for training purposes with the engineering branch of the RAF.

By September 1942, DP845 had been fully transformed into the prototype of the Spitfire F.XII. (C P Russell Smith Collection)

Spitfires for the Many

The Spitfire F.XIV and F.XVIII

Although the initial Griffon-powered version of the Spitfire had not been an outstanding success it had proved quite convincingly that the concept of a higher-powered development of the basic marque would be of positive benefit. The original Griffon 61 engine had been a single-stage supercharged unit that had given the Spitfire Mk.XII excellent performance at low to medium level; yet, high level air combat was still the province of the Merlin-powered Spitfire Mk.IX. Although both the engine and aircraft had been a hasty marriage; design work was already in hand to develop the Griffon and to produce an airframe to match.

The first inklings of a Griffon with a two-stage supercharger became apparent in 1943 when engineers at Rolls Royce began bench testing the first development version. As it had shown such promise it was decided by the Air Ministry that Supermarine would provide six Spitfire Mk.VIIIs for test and development purposes, these being serialled JF316 to JF321, with JF317 the first to fly.

During flight testing the aircraft exhibited a spectacular turn of speed reaching 445 mph at 25,000 feet with a rate of climb that reached 5,000 feet per minute. The final aircraft from this batch, fitted with a Griffon 85 power unit, was dispatched to Rotol at Staverton for development of the contra-rotating propeller destined for the envisaged "Super Spitfire." This unit had two three-bladed propellers with contra-rotating shafts controlled by a single constant-speed unit.

Problems were experienced with these early contra propeller units. As designed, the Rotol pitch change mechanism controlled the front pro-

Spitfire Mk.XIV, RB140, was the first production aircraft. The first versions of this aircraft were based on the earlier Mk.VIII airframe, therefore they were of the high-backed variety. Prominent in this view are the wing-mounted Hispano cannons. (C P Russell Smith Collection)

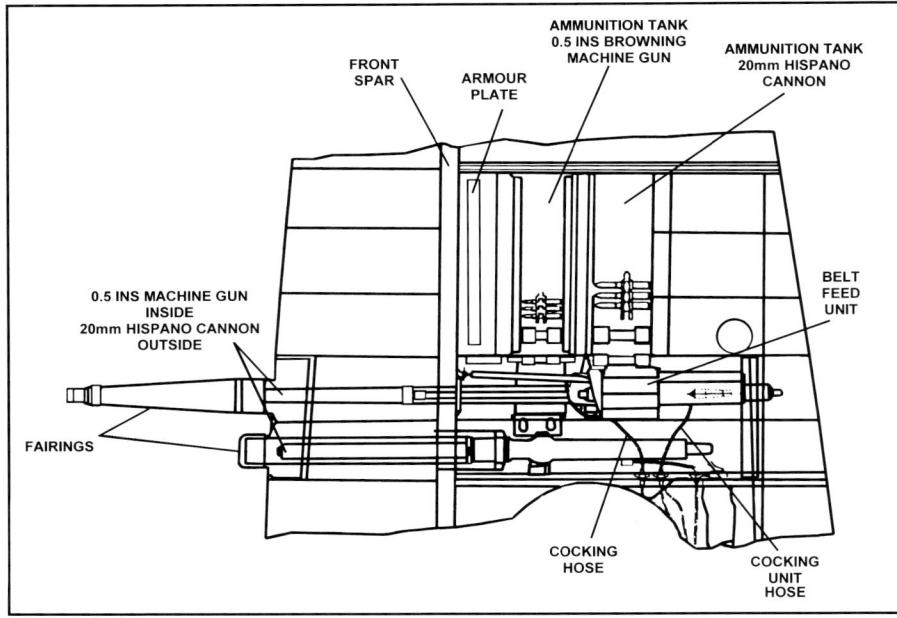

The cannon and machine gun installations were very similar in the later versions of the Spitfire, being based on the universal "E" wing. (Big Bird Aviation Collection)

peller with control of the rear propeller achieved by a transitional bearing. On at least one occasion this bearing failed accompanied by a very loud bang. The aircraft had been travelling at a speed of 400 mph. The resulting failure caused the Spitfire's top speed to drop dramatically to 130 mph. Fortunately for the pilot, the airfield of Middle Wallop was close by. Even though the throttle was fully advanced, the aircraft managed to maintain only enough forward airspeed to allow a landing with the flaps lowered at the last moment.

The preceding five airframes were all fitted with Griffon engines that drove five-bladed propeller units. In their new guise, whatever their intended role, all were designated as Spitfire Mk.XIV. Unfortunately, the fitment of the Griffon engine produced an overpowered aircraft that would have been unusable for front-line service. Therefore, further development was required. Changes were needed to the throttle box, the friction damper, and propeller control. Before these modifications were carried out, performance testing had revealed a top speed of 447 mph at an altitude of 25,600 feet dropping to 389 mph at 16,000 feet.

This first configuration of the type flew with the earlier version fin and broad chord pointed top rudder as installed on the greater majority of the production Mk.VIIIs. As the Griffon produced greater power and therefore more torque, a fin of larger area with a straightened leading

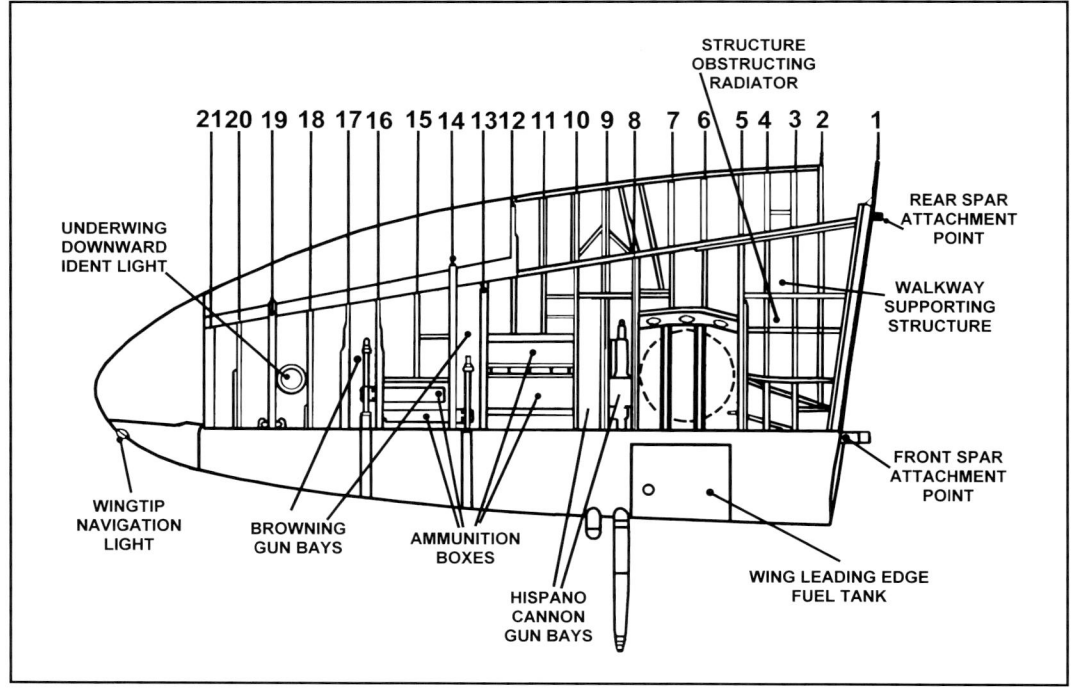

The wing structure of the Spitfire F.XIV and F.XVIII were very similar in construction although the latter were built using heavier gauge material in some areas thus giving greater overall strength. (Big Bird Aviation Collection)

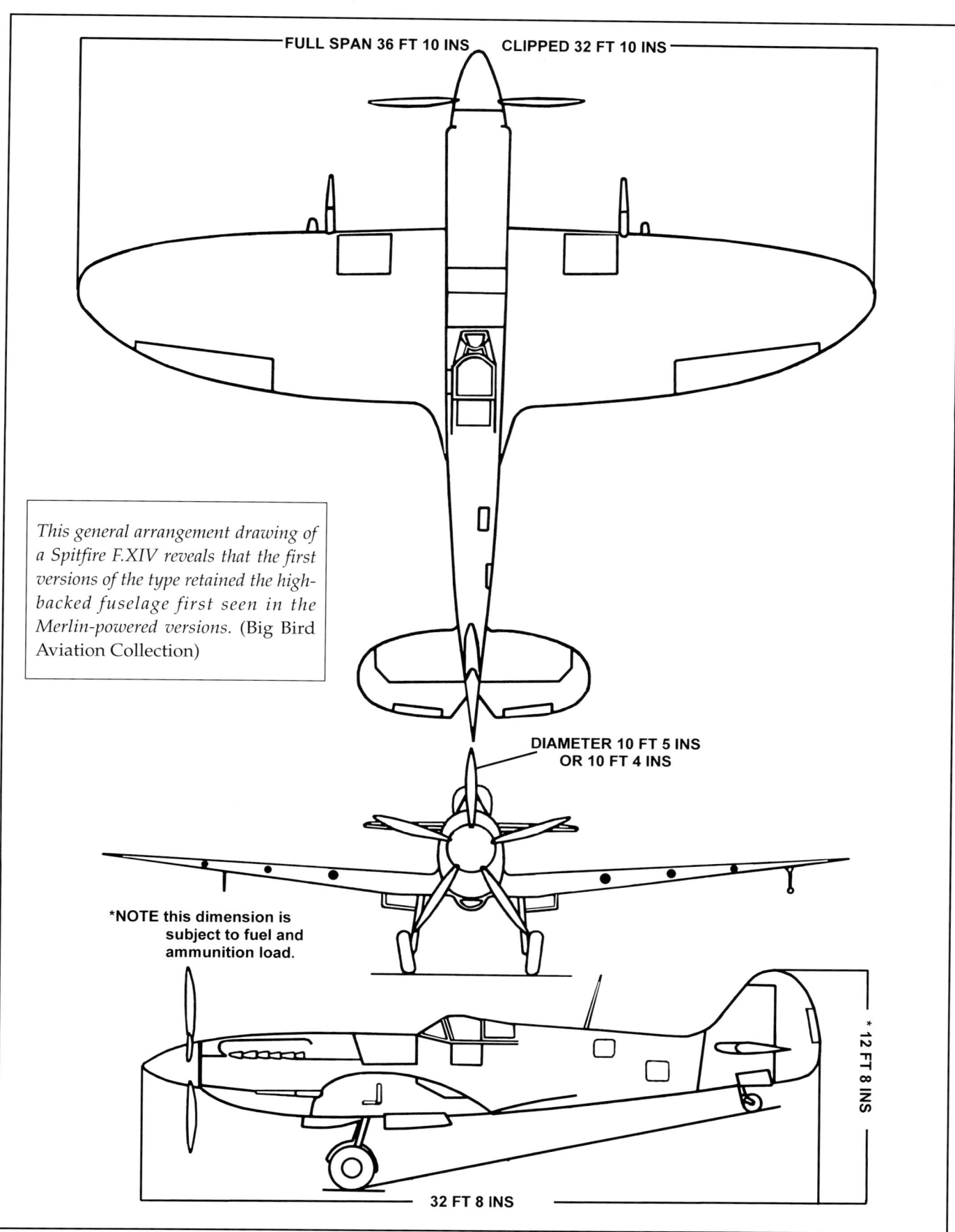

This general arrangement drawing of a Spitfire F.XIV reveals that the first versions of the type retained the high-backed fuselage first seen in the Merlin-powered versions. (Big Bird Aviation Collection)

Both the Spitfire F.XIV and F.XVIII were fitted with a five-blade propeller unit. This view under the spinner reveals the complex gearing required to change the pitch angle of the blades. (Chris Michell)

edge was fitted complete with a rudder that was even broader than that carried before.

Initial flight tests of the new marque revealed an aircraft of greater performance than previous versions of the Spitfire. However, the RAF and Fighter Command in particular required further test flights to define the parameters of the Mk.XIV. Therefore aircraft JF317 was dispatched to A&AEE for evaluation in conjunction with the AFDU at Wittering by the end of July 1943. Comparison flights were carried out against a Spitfire Mk.VIII powered by a Merlin 63.

The flight test report was to reveal that the Mk.XIV was slightly heavier on control feel, especially about the pitch axis. Spin handling had to be induced and instead of a normal stable nose down attitude the aircraft was subject to some oscillation although recovery was fairly quick upon release of the controls. Overall the new version was fairly normal in performance and behaviour, albeit the controls were heavier up to an altitude of 25,000 feet. Once past that point the Mk.XIV easily outstripped its Merlin-powered rival. In its final

To load the propeller unit onto the engine drive shaft requires the use of a block and tackle. Once installed, a main locking nut is torque-loaded onto the shaft using a very large spanner. To counteract the turn of the spanner, persons are required to apply an opposite force. (Chris Michell)

report, the A&AEE recommended the type for quantity production. This was eventually translated on a one-for-one basis in place of the Merlin-powered Mk. VIIIs already on order.

Described by Supermarine as the Type 369, the Spitfire Mk.XIV was authorised for production although some changes in handling were required before full RAF acceptance. Much of the airframe was derived from the Mk.VIII with strengthening at critical points to compensate for the increased engine power. The first production aircraft, RB140, was rolled out in September 1943 complete with an installed Griffon 65 engine and a five-bladed Rotol propeller. Fixed armament was a pair of 0.50-inch Browning machine guns matched to a pair of 20mm Hispano cannons in an "E" type wing. By this time the .303-inch bullet had been retired in favour of the more universally accepted half inch round.

Comparison flight testing between an Mk.XIV and a Spitfire Mk.IX was carried out by the AFDU which concluded that the Griffon-powered aircraft was a far better all-around performer than the earlier marque. Overall speed was increased by 25–35 mph whilst there was a corresponding increase in the climb-to-height ratio. Manoeuvrability was also better at all heights and speeds although all pilots were warned that care should be taken during taxiing and takeoff.

A further development of the basic fighter was to produce the FR.XIV. It featured increased fuel capacity in the rear fuselage which helped compensate for the type's initial shortage of range plus oblique and vertical cameras just aft of the cockpit. The increased weight necessi-

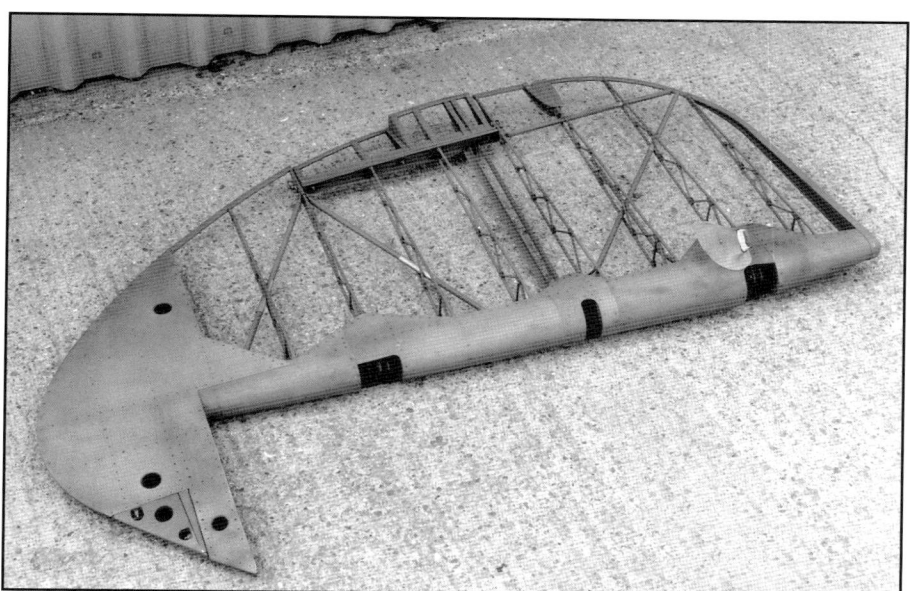

Under the skin of the broad chord rudder fitted to the main run of Griffon Spitfires. This example awaits skinning and balancing before fitment. (Chris Michell)

tated strengthened wing spars and parts of the fuselage allied to improved wheels and tyres and undercarriage legs.

Further design proposals included adaptations for the fighter-bomber role plus modifications to carry external long-range tanks. Changes to the engine oil feed system were also required. This resulted in the oil tank being relocated behind the fireproof bulkhead away from the engine. Not only did this mean that the powerplant was easily interchangeable, it also kept the lubricant away from the engine thus reducing the fire risk. A conse-

Seen from a slightly different angle the operating horns for the rudder show up quite clearly near the base of this newly-manufactured unit. (Chris Michell)

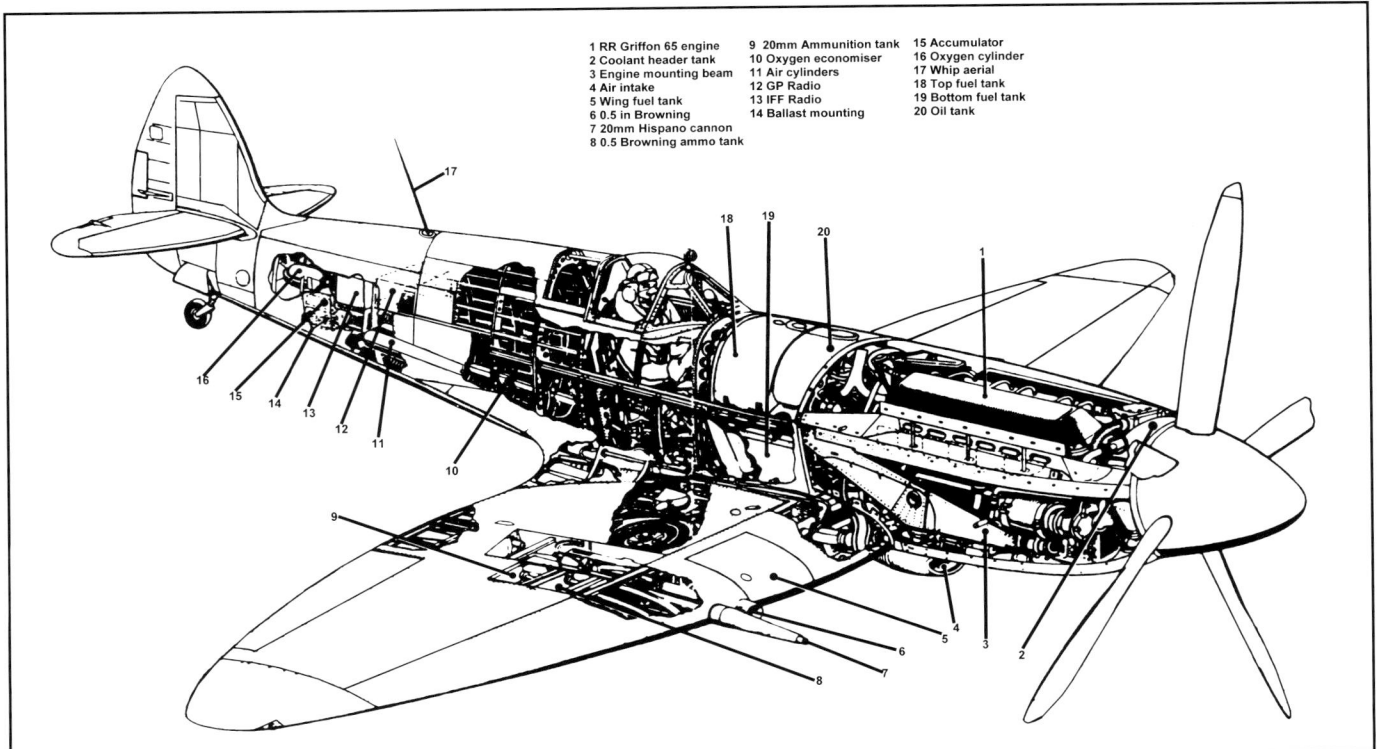

This cutaway of a Spitfire F.XIV reveals the location of the primary components within the airframe. (Eric B Morgan Collection)

quence of this modification was the reduced size of the top fuel tank which meant that its capacity decreased by 10–11 gallons. However, this smaller top fuel tank was not self sealing unlike the remainder of those installed in the airframe.

Fuel system control required the use of a five-way selector cock which replaced the plunger valve used on earlier marques of the Spitfire. Another innovation introduced with the Mk.XIV was a fuel low-level warning light which, on illumination, indicated that a total of 30 minutes powered flying time was left. As the engine fitted to this generation of the Griffon Spitfires was the largest fitted so far, an increase in underwing radiator size was required. Not only were the covers slightly longer, they also exhibited a greater depth. The primary radiator was that under the port wing whilst that under the starboard wing was concerned with keeping the lubrication system cooled.

The increase in engine power also brought about changes in maintenance procedures. Up to this point chocks on the main wheels had been more than sufficient to restrain the aircraft. The Griffon engine, with its greatly increased power output, changed all that. Proper reinforced tie-down points were built into the airframe whilst the chocks were redesigned to be bigger and were also capable of being connected by the use of tie bars. All were finally connected to a ground tie-down ring to which was lashed a strap around the rear fuselage to replace the earlier restraint of three men sitting on the tail. Prior to modification action, early ground runs quite frequently resulted in distortion of the fin leading edge after a period of running at full throttle.

Tests were also carried out to clear the marque for use with zero length rockets which were successful. As the war progressed, the RAF also proposed that an arrestor hook be fitted as well as Rocket Assisted Take Off Gear (RATOG) for operation from unimproved airfields in Europe.

Extensive test flights with aircraft fitted with standard wingtips revealed that the high-stress loads imposed by manoeuvring caused extensive wrinkling of the skin on the wings. Although Supermarine insisted that the deformation was not serious, the RAF decided that all production aircraft would be flown with clipped wings thus reducing wing stress.

As the Mk.XIV design progressed, results of combat reports were made available to the team at Supermarine. One of the prime requirements was improved all-around visibility which was solved by reducing the height of the rear fuselage and replacing the sliding canopy with a bubble hood canopy. This new production version was then designated F.Mk.XIVe although the mounts for reconnaissance cameras were incorporated from the outset.

Further test flights revealed that the clear hood was experiencing problems on release. Specifically, that on jettison the departing canopy was striking the rear fuselage quite savagely before badly damaging the fin. Another problem that continued to plague operational aircraft was the wrinkling of the upper wing surface which was concentrated in the area of the wing bay upper access panel. Curing this fault was finally resolved by strengthening the end of the spanwise stringers under the upper skin. Thereafter, except for airframe overstress, the upper wing wrinkling problem virtually disappeared.

In order to extend the capabilities of the Spitfire, an FR.XIVe was dispatched in 1946 to Royal Canadian Air Force (RCAF) Station Namao Canada. It underwent winterisation trials under the aegis of the Ministry of Supply (MoS) Winterisation Experimental Establishment. This aircraft, TZ138, was later sent to Fort Churchill for a series of tests.

During one of a series of flights the aircraft was required to land for refuelling at a small rudimentary strip named "Le Pas." Upon completion, the aircraft began to taxi out for take-off when the surface of the snow gave way and the propeller tips were damaged. Once the propeller had been replaced, the problem of removing the Spitfire to a more substantial airfield remained. To combat this, a set of Tiger Moth skis were temporarily attached. On rotate the skis dropped clear, allowing the undercarriage to retract normally. Although not recommended for normal use by single-engined fighters, they were cleared for emergency disposable use. Once the aircraft finished its service life it was sold to a series of civilian owners and now resides at Van Nuys.

As this version of the Spitfire was developed it underwent some radical changes. This particular airframe has a cut down rear fuselage with a bubble canopy. This aircraft is being used to trial test an under-fuselage fuel tank. (C P Russell Smith Collection)

Possibly the most important structural component in the Spitfire is Frame 5 which not only acts as the engine mount and firewall, but also as the front spar mount. The one on the left requires restoration whilst that on the right is a newly-built example. (Chris Michell)

The problem of longitudinal stability resulted in one aircraft, RM784, being allocated for development flight trials. Airborne handling with a fabric-covered rudder revealed a good degree of stability. However, installation of the normal metal rudder plus connected trim tab produced exactly the opposite although disconnecting and locking off the tab showed some improvements.

After many hours of extensive flight testing at Boscombe Down, the AFDU at Wittering, and flying at the Central Fighter Establishment at Tangmere, the Spitfire Mk.XIV and its various subvariants were cleared for operational service. Basic technical data for the type included a span of 36 feet 10 inches with a gross area of 242 square feet. Wing loading was set at 35 pounds per square feet. Fuselage length was 32 feet 8 inches.

Powerplants installed throughout the life of the aircraft included the Griffon 61 rated at 1,785 hp and the Griffon 85 rated at 2,055 hp both of which were started using a Coffman cartridge starter.

The fuel system contained a basic load of 109 gallons with overload options of 30, 45, 50, 90, and 170 gallons in external tanks. Published performance figures for the Spitfire Mk.XIV revealed a top speed of 439 mph at 24,500 feet with a maximum diving speed of 470 mph. Weapons installed in the first batches of aircraft included the "B" wing with a pair of cannons plus four machine guns. The later versions had the "E" wing which featured two cannons with the machine gun complement reduced to two. Range for the basic fighter version was set at 460 miles. The FR version had its range and endurance increased to 610 miles due to the extra fuel tanks in the rear fuselage.

Deliveries to the RAF began with No. 610 Sqdn (City of Chester) based at Exeter during the period January–February 1944. The following month saw deliveries increasing thus allowing No. 91 Sqdn and No. 322 (Dutch) Sqdn as part of No. 85 Group to re-equip. All three units were fully *au fait* with the Spitfire by June of that year when the German forces began the bombardment of London using long-range V.1 Flying Bombs. This wing was also charged with intercepting and shooting down any high altitude reconnaissance aircraft dispatched by the Luftwaffe.

By increasing the engine fuel boost, the Spitfire XIVs operating alongside the units equipped with the Mk.XII were able to intercept and destroy these lethal weapons. By the end of September 1944 this bombardment had ended. As the invasion of Europe post–D-Day continued, further units began to convert to the marque. These included Nos. 130, 350 (Belgian), and 402 (Canadian) Sqdns, which as part of the No. 83 Group moved to France in support of operations there. Nos. 41 and 610 Sqdns eventually moved to Europe as part of No. 83 Group where they were to encounter the Me-262 jet fighter.

Running parallel with the fighter deliveries were those of the fighter reconnaissance version complete with a single F.24 oblique camera that could be directed to port or starboard as required. The first units in the 2nd Tactical Air Force (No. 2 TAF) to receive the new aircraft were the Nos. 2 and the 430 Sqdns in November 1944. The first unit came from the No. 35 Wing whilst the latter had been part of the No. 39 Wing.

First operational sorties by both Squadrons were undertaken not long after re-equipping although they soon experienced trouble with intercepting Messerschmidt Me-262 fighters attempting to stop the Tac R missions taking place. From this point onward the Spitfire Mk.XIV remained the primary air superiority fighter with No. 2 TAF until the end of hostilities and for a short time afterward. No. 2nd TAF was one of those units allocated to the newly created British Armed Forces Overseas (BAFO) with which it remained until April 1947.

Deliveries to other theatres began in June 1945 with No. 11 Sqdn based in India. Although by the time the squadron had become fully operational, hostilities had ended. The type began to leave RAF service in 1946, finally disappearing in 1950.

Overall, 957 aircraft were produced through to the end of 1945. As the development of the Spitfire continued, the Mk.XIV was superseded by later versions. Therefore many of these aircraft were available for resale. In Europe, Belgium purchased 132 aircraft, although some of these were lost in a series of mysterious crashes for which no obvious reason was ever found, whilst a further 70 were handed over to the Royal Indian Air Force. Farther east the Royal Thai Air Force purchased 30 FR.XIVs for operational use, these included the zero-length rocket launch fixtures.

The next version of the Griffon Spitfire to leave the drawing board was the Mk.XVIII. Yet again the aircraft was based on the fuselage of the earlier Mk.VIII although it would require extensive modification to cope with the increased power of the proposed version. To improve the airborne handling of the new aircraft, a redefinition of the wing's aerodynamic form was proposed.

Another change to the wing was the method of spar construction, as a solid spar was used instead of the earlier method of laminating square tubular booms together. This made for a stronger assembly overall. Since there was an increase in fuel capacity the opportunity was taken

Frame 5 is seen from the cockpit side where the number of fitment mountings is few. Note the quality of the workmanship. (Chris Michell)

The front face of Frame 5 reveals the mounting points for the Griffon engine plus ancillary components. (Chris Michell)

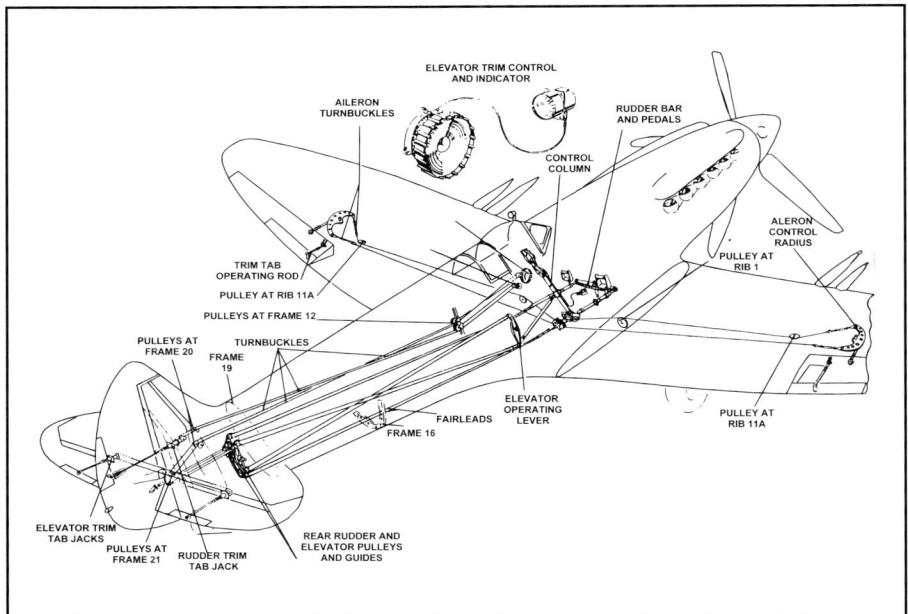

The Spitfire F.XIV and the Spitfire F.XVIII had a very similar flying control system installed. In common with many cable-operated aircraft the start of the runs for the rudder and elevators were rods which assisted in the adjustment/setting up process. (NATO AM)

to increase the strength of the main undercarriage units. Although there was some increase in weight with this new variant, the handling and top speed remained much the same. The version of engine installed in the Mk.XVIII was the same as that of the earlier marque, the Griffon 65.

Designated by Supermarine as the Type 394, the new version had a bubble canopy from the outset plus installation fixtures for F.24 or F.52 cameras, some of which were protected by canvas curtains that allowed camera bay heating to be installed for high altitude work.

The Mk.XVIII was seen as a development of the preceding Mk.XIV, therefore it was deemed that no special prototypes would be required. The first production aircraft, SM843, was dispatched to the trials airfield at High Post during June 1945. This airframe had two F.24 cameras in the rear fuselage plus a fuel tank. As the all-up weight had increased again, the undercarriage legs and wing mounts were yet again strengthened to cope with the increased load.

The first test flight of the Spitfire revealed a longitudinal stability problem plus unacceptable propeller vibration. The latter was cured by replacing the propeller unit whilst the former was reduced by installing a broader chord rudder and split trim tab. Further flight trials were carried out at A&AEE and the AFDU where tactical development was the requirement.

Deliveries to the RAF began with SM844 on 28 May 1945 when No. 28 Sqdn based in Hong Kong received its operational complement. A total of 300 airframes were produced. They consisted of 201 fighter reconnaissance versions plus 99 pure fighter bombers. This latter version was built without reconnaissance fitments and featured mountings for wing-mounted bombs and rockets. As with the earlier Mk.XIV, this version was also trialled with an arrestor hook and RATOG gear for operating from unprepared airfields. The trials were successful, but the installation was not continued past the handful converted.

Supermarine also attempted to extend the type's usage postwar by proposing a two-seat trainer version which was not pursued. Another novel use for the Mk.XVIII was as a target tug. Complete with winch and the required controls, aircraft SM970 was tested at Farnborough and Lasham. To ensure that the winch cable would not become entangled with the retractable tail wheel, a guard was fitted. This particular experiment was not continued any further since the RAF decided to purchase conversions of the Tempest TT.5 for the role. Although the Mk.XVIII was intended to replace the earlier Mk.XIV the cessation of hostilities resulted in the mass cancellation of outstanding production contracts.

All in-service use by the RAF was located overseas, none being operated by units in the UK. In Singapore, No. 60 Sqdn at Seletar received the Mk.XVIII in 1947. Further units in the Far East, Nos. 11, 28, and 81 Sqdns, also received the new Spitfire. Whilst in the Middle East, No.32 Sqdn and No. 208 Sqdn received a mix of fighter bomber and fighter reconnaissance versions. The outbreak of hostilities in Malaya saw Nos. 28 and 60 Sqdns carry out anti-terrorist attacks against communist insurgents.

Further action became the lot of No. 32 and 208 Sqdns during 1947 when clashes occurred between the Arabs and the Jews as the State of

Israel was established. During this period the aircraft of both squadrons were suffering a series of unserviceabilities due to propeller blade root shrinkage as the wood used in their manufacture contracted in the heat.

In the early hours of 22 May 1948 the peace of both squadrons was shattered by the dropping of two bombs on the airfield at Ramat David. Two of No. 32 Sqdn's aircraft were destroyed in the ensuing blaze. Prior to departing, the attacking aircraft, by now identified as Spitfires, flew the length of the airfield strafing as they went. A further attack took place later that day although this time aircraft of No. 208 Sqdn were waiting to intercept. The three attackers, all from the Royal Egyptian Air Force (REAF), were destroyed in the combat that followed.

Even further action followed No. 208 Sqdn in 1950 when it was deployed to Khartoum in support of ground forces searching out and destroying insurgent bands that were infiltrating Eritrea from Ethiopia. As well as combat sorties, the Spitfires were also used in the postal role and for the aerial delivery of small spare parts for Army units.

As the requirement for the Mk.XVIII had decreased by the end of hostilities, the greater majority of aircraft were dispatched to various maintenance units. From here they were later sold to other air forces or were scrapped with very few flying hours on the clock. Countries receiving supplies included the Royal Indian Air Force with 20 airframes. A small order consisting of just three aircraft was sold to the Union of Burma Air Force during April 1948.

Technical details for the F.XVIII are a span of 36 feet 10 inches with a surface area of 242 square feet. As the All Up Weight (AUW) had increased, the wing loading had proportionally risen to 36.6 pounds per square foot. Fuselage length was 32 feet 8 inches as before. Powerplants installed in this variant included the Griffon 65 rated at 2,035 hp whilst later airframes were equipped with the Griffon 67 rated at 2,375 hp. Both were started on the ground using a Coffman cartridge starter. Fuel contents within the airframe were 175 gallons plus overload tanks capable of carrying 30, 45, 50, and 90 gallons respectively.

Maximum speed was 437 mph at 24,500 feet. Armament was installed in a standard "E" wing and consisted

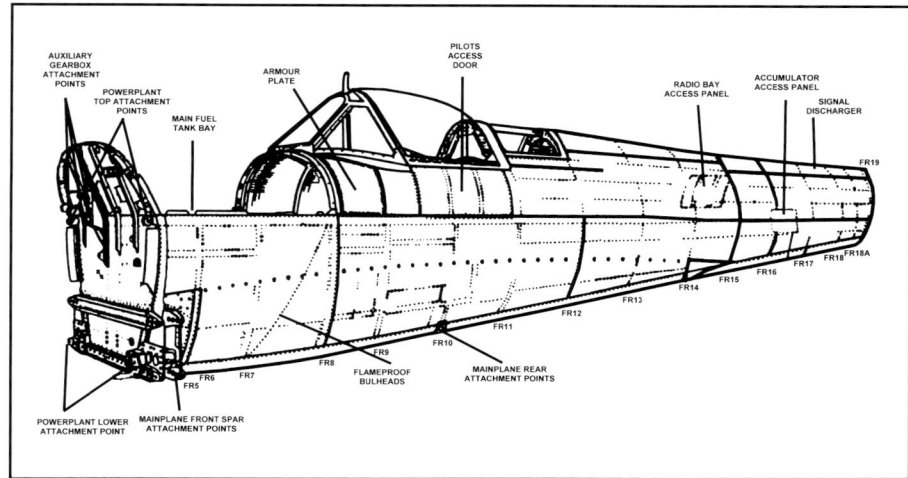

This external diagram reveals the layout of the fuselage skin plating. Much was 22 SWG in thickness although some areas were 20 SWG in thickness. Armour plate was installed in the areas of greatest vulnerability. (NATO AM)

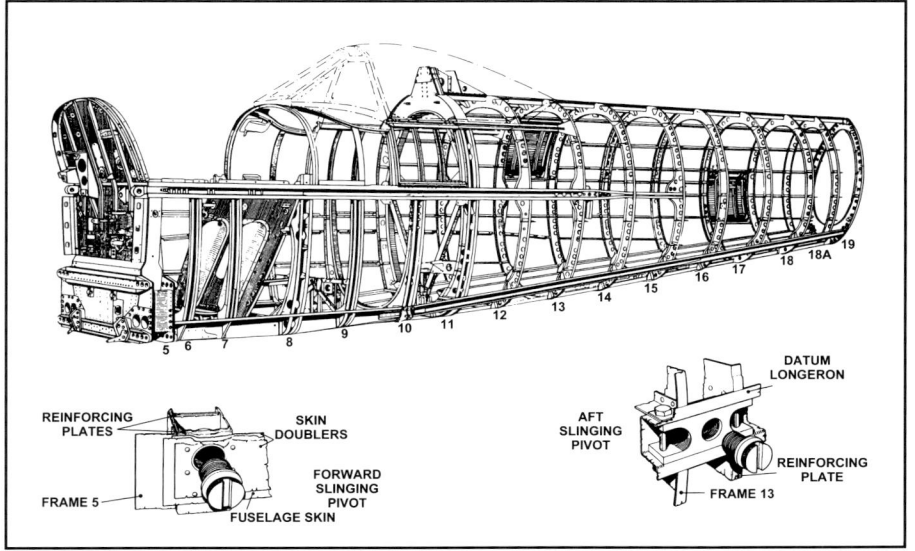

The structure underneath the skin could trace its ancestry back to the prototype airframe K5054. Major differences were wrought upon the various components where wartime experience had shown it to be required. (Big Bird Aviation Collection)

Seen in this side-on view is Spitfire FR.XVIII, SM843, which spent its whole life as a test and trials aircraft. Prominent is the camera window located to the rear of the bubble canopy. (Eric B Morgan Collection)

of a pair of cannons and machine guns. Bombs up to a maximum of 500 pounds could also be carried as could a selection of underwing rocket projectiles. The camera installation could consist of one F.24 with a focal length of 14 inches or a pair of F.24 cameras of 20 inches focal length or an F.52 vertically mounted unit.

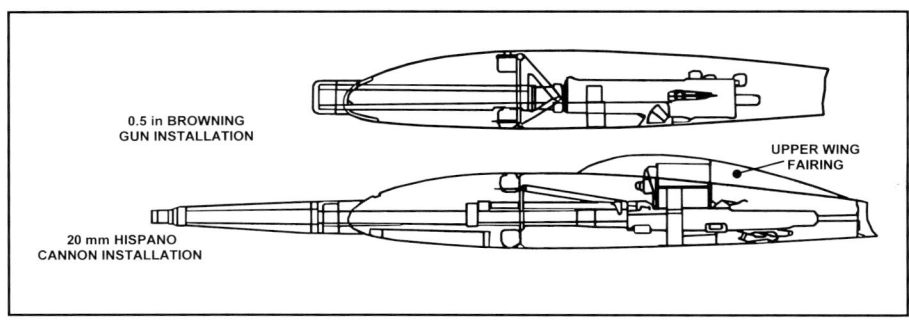

The through section of the gun bays (above) in the Spitfire F.XIV/XVIII reveals the breech blister is the only protuberance to disturb the smooth lines of the wing. (Big Bird Aviation Collection)

This Spitfire F.XVIII is photographed in mid-1945 prior to delivery to the Royal Air Force. The similarity between this and the earlier F.XIV is readily apparent although the airframe of this particular variant was of a far stronger construction. (C P Russell Smith Collection)

This side-on view of MV293 shows the broad chord rudder and redesigned fin fitted to the main batch of Griffon-engined Spitfires. The profile of the rear fuselage and the shape of the canopy can be seen clearly. (Nick Challoner)

From this angle the wings and general demeanour of the Spitfire FR.XIV are clearly revealed. This particular example is the preserved MV293. (Damien Burke)

This operational Spitfire FR.XIV is allocated to the No. II Sqdn. Of note is the relaxed attitude of the controls, the open cockpit entry hatch, and the prominent camera window. (C P Russell Smith Collection)

Close observation of the underwing of this Spitfire F.XVIII, TP197, reveals that this is a fighter version as it is fitted with underwing rocket projectile mounts. (C P Russell Smith Collection)

Supermarine Spitfire FR.XVIII, TP386, is undergoing maintenance at the Maintenance Unit at Nicosia, Cyprus. Of note are the prominent mounting beams for the Griffon engine. (C P Russell Smith Collection)

In concert with the high-backed versions of the F.XIV, the Belgian Air Force also operated examples of the low-backed Spitfire FR.XIV. This is a training unit aircraft assigned to the Operational Training Unit at Coxyde. Wearing serial SG-105, this airframe has blocked cannon ports. (C P Russell Smith Collection)

This view of a Belgian Air Force Spitfire FR.XIV reveals the size of the five-bladed propeller fitted to this variant. Of note are the missing cannons exemplified by the open stub mounts. (C P Russell Smith Collection)

Prominent in this shot of SG-72, a Spitfire F.XIV of the Belgian Air Force, are the bulges required to cover the increased size of the Griffon powerplant. (C P Russell Smith Collection)

The Belgian Air Force also modified some of its Spitfire F.XIVs with improvised camera ports as seen here. The bulges on the wings cover the Hispano cannon breeches. (C P Russell Smith Collection)

This posed gate guard is a Spitfire FR.XIVc on duty at RAF Cosford. Close observation of the aircraft reveals many of the skin panel lines and the painted-over oblique camera port. (Ray Deacon)

Spitfire in the Blue

The Spitfire PR.19

This, the final reconnaissance variant of the Spitfire, was an amalgam of the best parts from all the previous versions of this fine aircraft. The issued Air Staff Requirement, Specification No. 475, had been proposed in response to a real need for an improved high altitude reconnaissance platform as the current incumbent in the role, the PR.XI, was used for missions far removed from its original task. This had encompassed solo high speed photo runs at low to medium altitudes thus the need for such esoteric items as cabin pressurisation had not been a requirement. Also, the installed Merlin 61 and 63 engines fitted to the greater majority of these aircraft could not deliver the power necessary to maintain a climb to such heights. An attempt to combat this deficiency was to install the boosted R-R Merlin 70 in a few airframes plus a pressure cabin. This was seen as a stopgap as altitudes for reconnaissance rose to a requirement far in excess of 40,000 feet.

By the time this need had arisen the Griffon engine was already powering fighter and fighter reconnaissance versions of the Spitfire and had revealed the extra power needed for such a requirement was available. The new version was allocated the Supermarine Type numbers 389 for the preliminary batch and 390 for the main production run, although the Air Ministry had decided to designate the aircraft the PR.XIX. This was later changed to PR.19 when Roman numeral designations were abandoned as unwieldy for everyday use.

Components included within the design came from various aircraft. The Spitfire PR.XI provided the wings with spars built to Directorate of Technical Development (DTD) Specification 273 for greater strength and structural rigidity which reduced the torsional twist of the earlier, lighter structures. The fighter Mk.XIV was the source for the undercarriage mounting pintles as well as the cooling and oil lubrication systems.

An extra not fitted to the first 22 production airframes was the provision for an additional 20 gallons of fuel housed in bag tanks in each wing although this was later a standard fitment in the remainder. Deletion of the armament also allowed a further 66 gallons of fuel to be housed in the normal wing leading edge tanks. Further fuel capacity was also provided in the space between the wing spars vacated by the cannons on the fighter and the wing cameras on the Merlin reconnaissance aircraft. Another tank was installed in the wing interspar space which contained 19 gallons. The final total of fuel in the airframe finally reached a capacity of 252 gallons. This is a marked contrast to the Spitfire Mk.I whose total capacity was 85 gallons.

As the task allocated to the PR.19 was very dangerous, it was felt that as much assistance as possible should be given to the pilot in the management of the fuel system. In the case of interspar tanks, their contents were boosted by air pressure to the top fuselage fuel tank. This in turn was controlled by an internal float valve which ensured that the tank would remain full until the wing tanks were empty. The remaining wing tanks were fed by electrical booster pumps and were graced by their own contents gauges. The fuselage of the new

Wearing the codes of the Photo Reconnaissance Development Unit, this PR.19 was one of those manufactured with a pressure cabin and Lobelle canopy matched to a rounded windscreen. (C P Russell Smith Collection)

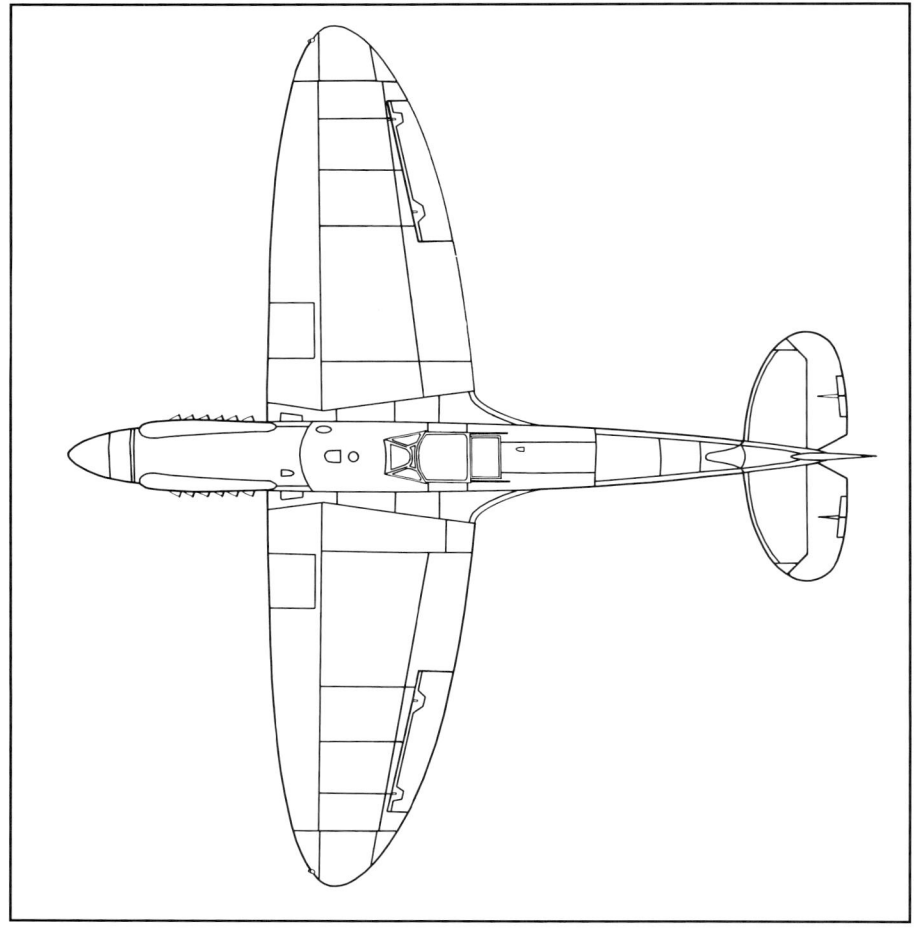

This Spitfire PR.19 was an amalgamation of numerous parts drawn from other versions of the aircraft. The influence of the closely-related Spitfire F.XIV can be seen quite clearly in this plan view. (Big Bird Aviation Collection)

marque was based on the Mk.XIV with the tail unit from the same airframe, but with adjustable ballast for trimming purposes.

As before, the first 22 aircraft were slightly different from the main production run. One of the primary differences was the canopy. The first batch had a standard canopy with a windscreen drawn from the PR.XI. The greater part of the production run had a pressure cabin installed and a reinforced Lobelle sliding hood. The main part of the production run featured a special type curved windscreen.

The cabin pressurisation system was based on that fitted to the high altitude interceptor Spitfire VII although the air intake and blower were relocated to the port side of the engine rather than the original installation on the starboard side of the Merlin-powered aircraft. When the cabin pressurisation system was not required it could be controlled by a spill valve for bypass purposes. Inflation of the hood seal was by use of a control valve in the cockpit as

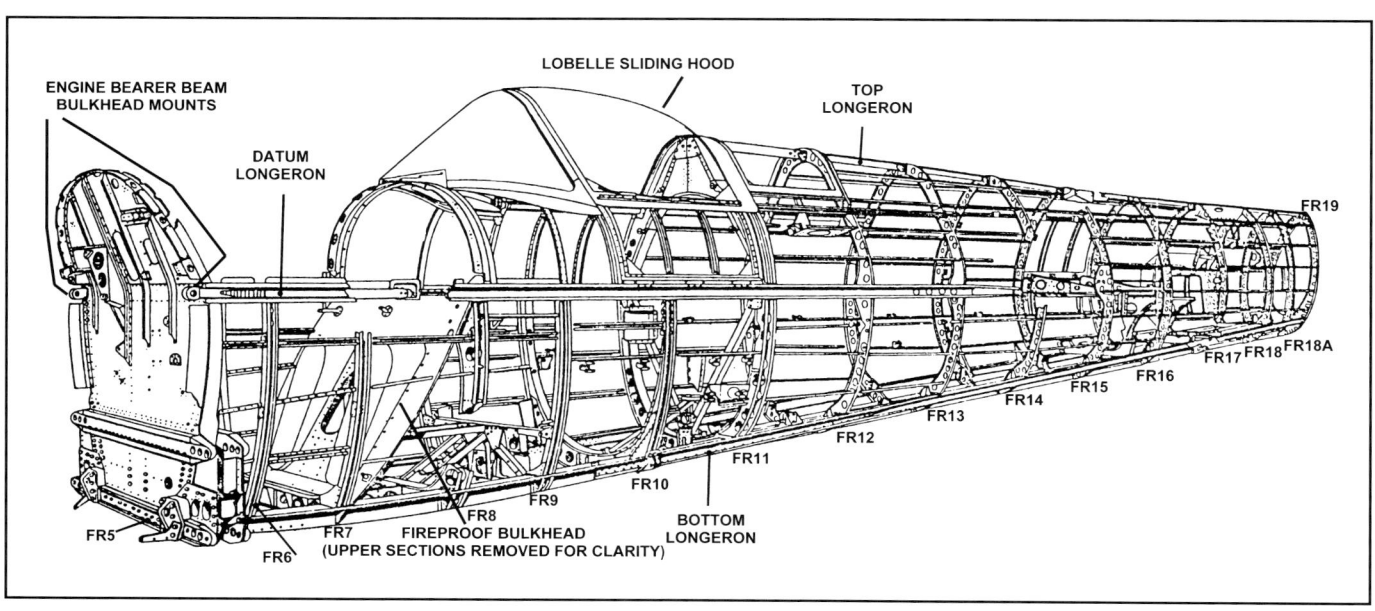

The fuselage of the Spitfire PR.19 was similar in strength and assembly to other versions of the high-backed Spitfires. (NATO AM)

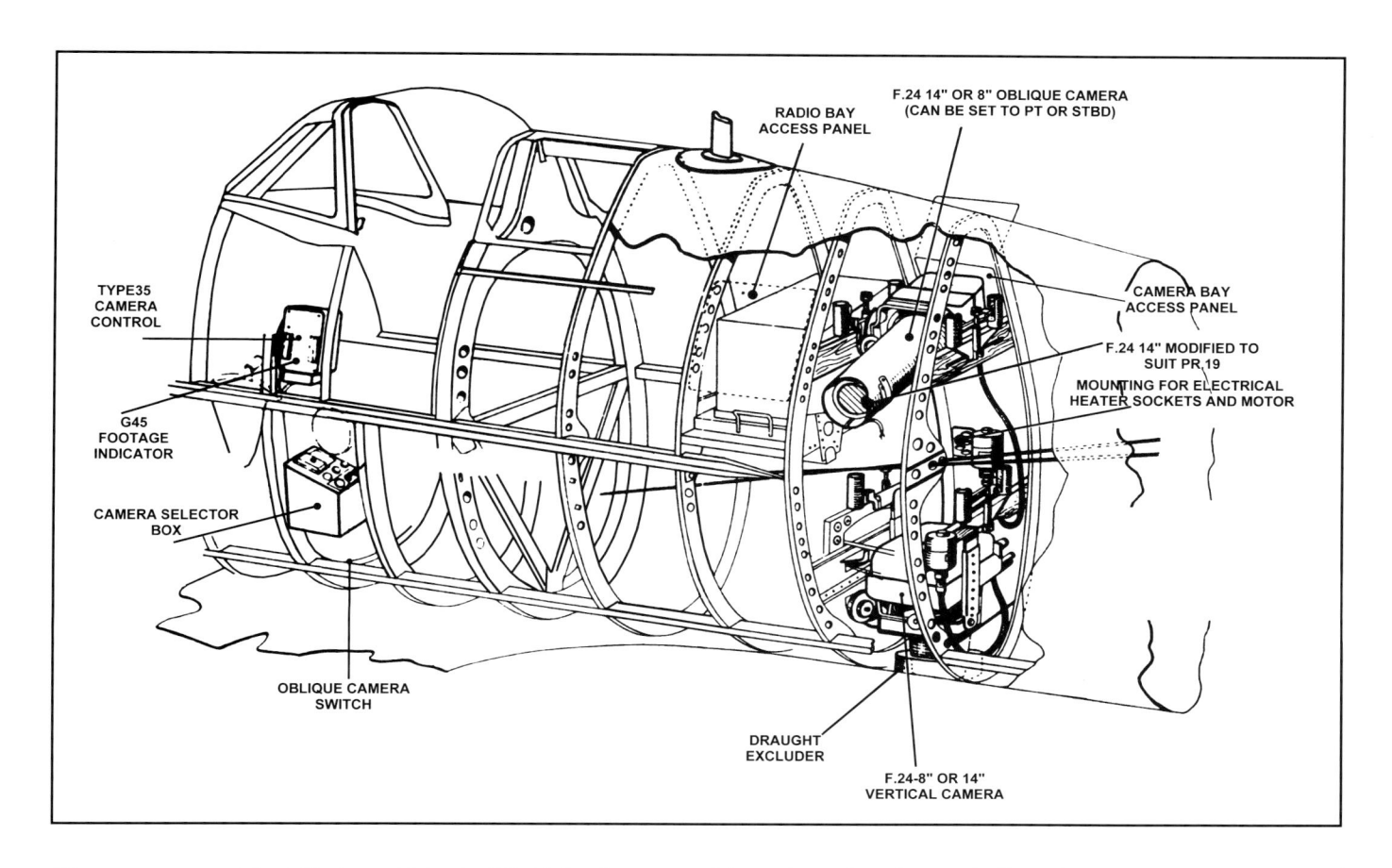

The camera mount installation within the PR.19 fuselage was of the universal variety and allowed numerous permutations of the available equipment. (Eric B Morgan Collection)

was the air demister system for the canopy and windscreen. To reduce the propensity of the pressure cabin to leak, special care was taken regarding the sealing of control run exits where they passed through the front and rear pressure bulkheads.

The cameras and their mounts were installed in the Universal Mounting assembly in the rear fuselage whilst the communications equipment was similar to that of the Mk.XIV fighter. The wing spar flange attachments were borrowed from the PR.XI for compatibility as were the wing leading edge tanks. The remainder of the fuel system was pure Mk.XIV in execution. Overload tanks were specified as a standard fit and encompassed the normal range available to the Spitfire and ranged in size from 30 gallons to 170 gallons.

The proposed powerplant was the Griffon 66 rated at 2,035 hp although the first 22 airframes were fitted with the Griffon 65 with a similar power rating. The Griffon 65 lacked the cabin blower unit, a heating system being fitted instead for pilot comfort. The method of engine mounting came from the Mk.XIV as did the cooling system. The propeller was the standard wooden five-bladed unit borrowed from the same aircraft.

Further technical details pertaining to the Spitfire PR.19 were a span of 36 feet 10 inches matched to a fuselage length of 32 feet 8 inches. The wing area of this variant was 242 square feet and the total internal fuel capacity was set at 254 gallons with provision for overload tanks rated at 30, 45, 90, and 170 gallons respectively. Normal performance parameters included a top speed of 445 mph at 26,000 feet with a range of 1,010 miles using only internal tank capacity. These figures were, of course, optimum and would not apply should the aircraft take off at its allowable maximum takeoff weight of 10,450 pounds.

As the Spitfire PR.19 was totally unarmed, its only defence was its height and its speed. To carry out its mission all the cameras were mounted in the fuselage Universal Mounting assembly. Examples of the setups possible included two F.52 of 36 inches focal length mounted vertically, or one F.52 vertically mounted. Another possible combination was a pair of cameras of the same type with focal lengths of 20 inches each fanned vertically whilst a pair of F.8 cameras of

Seen behind the canopy hood of a Spitfire PR.19 is the access panel for the ground power socket and the cover over the upper fuselage camera port. (Big Bird Aviation Collection)

20 inches focal length could be mounted in a similar manner. The final setup included a single F.24 camera mounted in the port oblique window with focal lengths of 4 inches or 8 inches as required. To ensure that the cameras and their windows remained clear, a warm air feed was tapped off from the rear of the starboard radiator and fed into two rigid ducts which took care of the upper fuselage installations whilst a further flexible pipe was directed to the lower fuselage windows.

As the RAF needed high-speed, high-altitude reconnaissance platforms in a hurry, the manufacturers proposed to deliver 16 PR.XI aircraft fitted with a pressure cabin and powered by a Merlin 63 engine. These in turn were followed by the 22 unpressurised PR.19 airframes whose serial range started at RM626. This airframe arrived for trials at the Supermarine test airfield at High Post on 27 April 1944. The first pressurised example was SW777 which arrived for testing at the same airfield in October of that year having been ordered in March. Deliveries of the first production aircraft began in May 1944.

The first test flights of the Photo Reconnaissance Unit (PRU) blue-bedecked PR.19 revealed an aircraft with some directional stability problems. These were exacerbated by the installation of an underfuselage overload tank. The test pilot did report, however, that the aircraft had potential. Further airborne evaluation was undertaken at RAF Benson with a 170-gallon ferry tank. Mid-air release of the tank was attempted during later trial flights although it hung up on the mountings when first attempted and required further development work to clear it for service use.

Extensive trials were undertaken at Boscombe Down where a variety of canopies and overload fuel tanks were put through their paces as were the fuel system and its gauging. Eventually the PR.19 was cleared to 40,000 feet with the external tanks drained fully to empty. During flight trials many pilots reported that the aircraft was longitudinally unstable during some parts of the flight enve-

The fin and rudder of the PR.19 are very similar to that fitted to the Griffon fighter versions. Prominent in this view is the rudder trim tab whose operating rod is also clearly shown. (Big Bird Aviation Collection)

lope with an overload tank although it behaved far better without. Further evaluation flights with a trial camera installation in the wings were undertaken in April 1946 at Eastleigh using PM655 although this was not adopted as a standard fitment.

A final total of 225 aircraft were produced for RAF service, although a number, some 170 in total, were cancelled due to the cessation of hostilities in Europe and the Far and Middle East theatres of operations. Whilst in service with the RAF, the operating organisation was initially Bomber Command and the PRU was based at Benson although some examples were in service with both Middle East and Far East Commands. The first unit to equip with the PR.19 was No. 542 Sqdn in June 1944, followed by No. 16 Sqdn in March 1945 which later became one of the primary postwar reconnaissance units within No. 2 TAF in West Germany.

The first operational sortie was undertaken on 25 May 1944 over the harbour and local defences at Le Havre using aircraft RM628, a Griffon 65-powered aircraft. Other units that flew the PR.19 included Nos. 34 and 81 Sqdns which provided much needed reconnaissance and meteorological capabilities in the Far East.

Some of these airframes later had their upper fuselage portions painted in light grey in an effort to reduce the heat buildup in the camera compartment within the fuselage, thus reducing the possible damage to the films and their magazines. This problem did not affect units based in Europe where the climate was far more temperate in nature.

Other units associated with the Spitfire PR.19 included No. 34 Sqdn in

The tail wheel assembly of the PR.19 is enclosed by a pair of retractable doors as are those of the other Griffon-powered aircraft. (Big Bird Aviation Collection)

The retractable tail wheel borrowed from the F.VIII was also installed in the Griffon fighters and the PR.19. (Big Bird Aviation Collection)

Seen from the front the starboard main gear reveals its tie down points more clearly. The radiator behind the undercarriage leg has a filter fitted to reduce debris entering the system. (Big Bird Aviation Collection)

the UK whilst the forces in Germany also boasted No. 2, 16, and 54 Sqdns. Although their usage of the type was fairly short-lived, by the time of their re-equipment with newer aircraft during 1950 they had been allocated to the newly created BAFO. However, the units that must bear the record for the shortest operational use of an aircraft are Nos. 681, 682, and 683 Sqdns which served in the Far East, France, and Italy respectively for a period of only a few months.

No. 81 Sqdn was to achieve a small measure of fame when it undertook the last operational reconnaissance flight of the type on 1 April 1954 using airframe PS888 operating out of the RAF base at Seletar, Singapore. This airframe flew in a totally unpainted state. This unit was also to lay claim to the greatest height and speed attained by a Spitfire and piston-powered aircraft generally.

On 5 February 1952, PR.19 PS852 was scheduled to undertake a meteorological flight to measure outside air temperatures and other weather phenomena at 5,000-foot increments. Eventually the aircraft levelled out at 50,000 feet actual height which equalled 48,500 feet indicated. Although the controls were very touch sensitive the pilot realised that a further increase in altitude might be possible. Eventually, an actual height of 51,500 feet was achieved although by this time the aircraft was virtually uncontrollable. During the Spitfire's occasionally out-of-control descent, the aircraft managed to achieve an indicated speed of 575 mph. Further investigation using the collected barometric data revealed that PS852 had reached a true altitude of 51,500 feet and a maximum speed of 690 mph, Mach 0.94.

In the UK the primary operator was 1 PRU based at RAF Benson which had introduced the genre to the RAF in the first place. To train pilots in the use of the Spitfire PR.19, No. 237 Operational Conversion Unit (OCU) came into existence in July 1947 and remained active until 1956

This rear view shot of the port underwing radiator clearly shows the reduction in exit space when the radiator flap is retracted. (Big Bird Aviation Collection)

when it re-equipped with Canberra bombers and T.4 trainers at its Bassingbourn base. Other training units such as No. 203 Advanced Flying School (AFS) and No. 61 Operational Training Unit (OTU) also used the aircraft in small quantities for a short period of time.

After the war there was a general rundown of Spitfire assets within the RAF which resulted in some PR.19s declared surplus to requirements before they had even entered service. These aircraft were later dispersed to Sweden although the original ordered total of 70 was later reduced to 50. The Indian Air Force also received 12 aircraft in 1948, enough to equip two squadrons dedicated to the reconnaissance task. A far smaller total, four in all, were later sold to the Royal Thai Air Force in early 1954. One surprise allocation was to the United States Army Air Force (USAAF) which operated two PR.19s, PM536 and 541, from Cairo during the closing stages of the war.

Later postwar operations using the PR.19 centred around the Temperature and Humidity (THUM) flight based at Woodvale, Lancashire, where the last ever operational Spitfire flight was undertaken on 9 May 1957 using aircraft PS853. This unit had been formed in response to an Air Ministry contract in 1951. This had been awarded to Short Brothers at Hooton Park near Liverpool.

Using three Spitfire PR.19s, the initial premise for the flight was all-weather meteorological flying. Originally, this location was the home to two other Spitfire units. However, when they replaced their piston fighters with the Gloster Meteor it was decided to move the THUM flight across the River Mersey to link up with another two Spitfire units

The elevators of the PR.19 were fitted with trim tabs and featured balance horns in the forward section. Also visible in this view is the tail navigation light on the rudder. (Big Bird Aviation Collection)

thus reducing the logistics costs. The primary task for the flight eventually settled on gathering information about weather behaviour up to altitudes of 30,000 feet. On 14 June 1957 the Spitfires were finally retired to be replaced by De Havilland (DH) Mosquito TT.35s.

The ailerons fitted to the Griffon Spitfires were mounted on bearings in contrast to the hinging previously used. Close observation of the wing skin reveals the smooth finish and high standard of flush riveting. (Big Bird Aviation Collection)

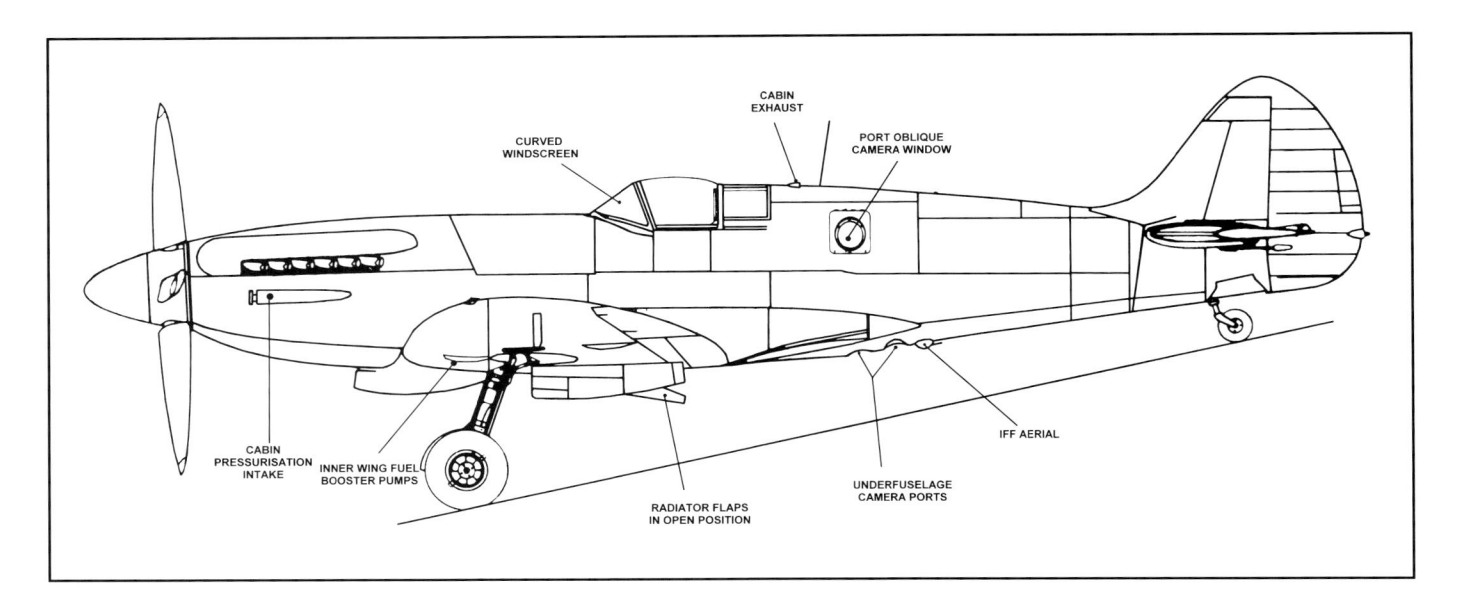

From the side, the PR.19 is virtually indistinguishable from the high-backed Griffon-powered fighters. Only the lack of wing armament and the cabin pressurisation intake fitted to the main production batch betray the differences. (Big Bird Aviation Collection)

After retirement these airframes became part of the Battle of Britain Flight based at Biggin Hill. Still part of this historic flight, Spitfire PR.19 PS853 moved to Binbrook where it carried out one unusual and last operational task for the frontline RAF. Here it was used for training Lightning pilots atop their jet-powered Mach 2 mounts to chase the P-51 Mustang fighters of the Indonesian Air Force during the period of the Malaysian confrontation.

Overall these mock combats revealed that the Lightning had a significant edge as long as it remained clear of a close entanglement where the tighter turning circle of its more nimble component would outfly the modern aircraft. The final tactic settled on was for the Lightning to approach the enemy fighter from underneath and enter the missile engagement zone without being observed before launching its infrared homing Firestreak missile.

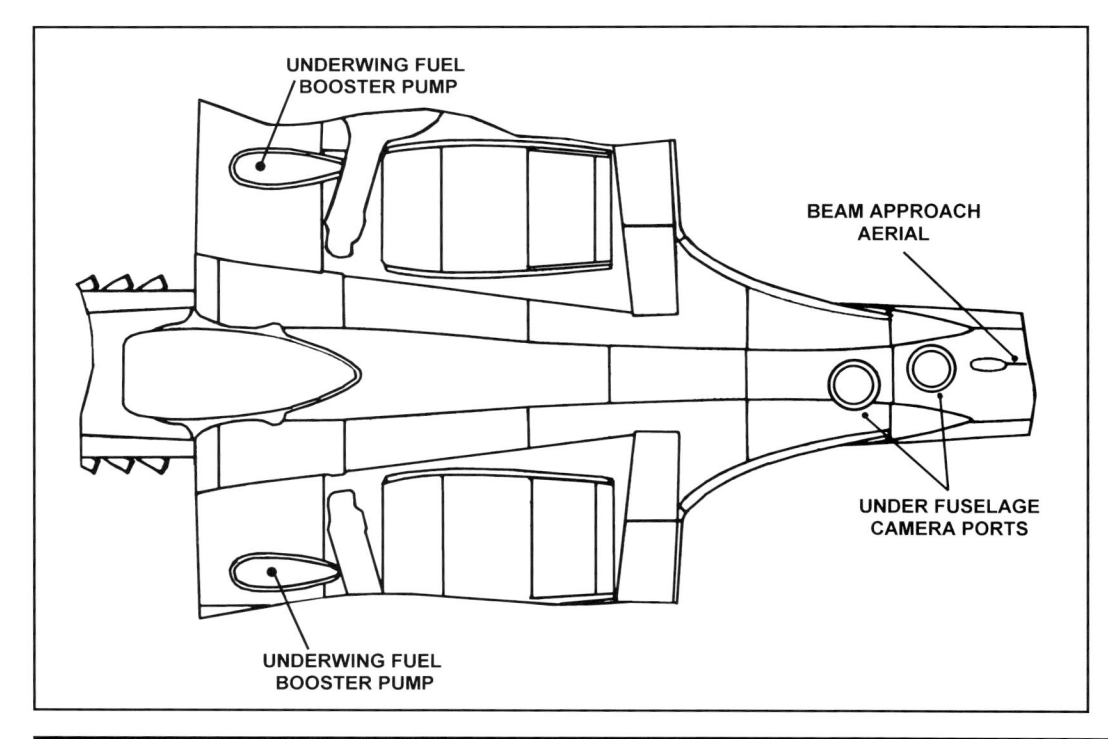

This section of the underneath of the Spitfire PR.19 clearly shows the layout of the camera ports and the blisters that cover the wing fuel tank pumps. (Big Bird Aviation Collection)

The Spitfire PR.19 was built in two versions, one unpressurised and one pressurised. This is the cabin intake of the pressurised version. (Big Bird Aviation Collection)

The propeller fitted to the PR.19 was of the five-bladed variety. Note the angle of the blade tips. (Big Bird Aviation Collection)

Seen in close up are the exhaust ports of a Griffon engine plus the fasteners that hold the access panels in place. (Big Bird Aviation Collection)

A handful of retired Spitfire PR.19s are still flying in private hands. This view of PM631 clearly reveals the curved windscreen unique to this version. (Dave Stewart)

This underwing shot of a PR.19 in the vicinity of the main gear bay shows quite clearly the housing for the wing tank fuel pump. (Big Bird Aviation Collection)

The open access panel in this PR.19 reveals the aft wall of the camera bay plus some of the fuselage structure. (Chris Michell)

With all the internal coverings removed, the cockpit structure is revealed. Of note are the aileron operating cables connected to the control column pulley. (Chris Michell)

This is Frame 11 inside a PR.19, most other versions of the Spitfire are similar. The pipe visible at the bottom of the fuselage is that for the camera bay heating. (Chris Michell)

Looking forward inside the PR.19 camera bay reveals the port fuselage camera window plus some of the operating system connections. (Chris Michell)

Although photographed in its days as a gate guard at RAF Benson, PS915 eventually returned to flying duties with the RAF BBMF. Close inspection of the fuselage reveals the edges of the skin panels. (Eric B Morgan Collection)

In landing condition, Spitfire PR.19, PM631, approaches for touchdown with both wing and radiator flaps fully deployed. (Nick Challoner)

This photo of Spitfire PR.19, RM632, shows it lacks the intake beneath the exhaust bank for the cabin pressurisation system, thus revealing it was one of the first built. (C P Russell Smith Collection)

After their service with the RAF, some Spitfire PR.19s entered service with foreign air forces. This particular airframe is pictured in the inventory of the Royal Thai Air Force. The novel rudder clamp should be noted. (C P Russell Smith Collection)

This underneath view of a Spitfire PR.19 clearly reveals the fairings for the wing fuel booster pumps and the under fuselage camera ports. (C P Russell Smith Collection)

Sitting on the pan at Woodvale, this Spitfire PR.19 awaits its final sortie on behalf of THUM Flight before retirement. (Big Bird Aviation Collection)

Caught just after liftoff, this PR.19 is just retracting its undercarriage, although the radiator flaps are still fully open. (Dave Stewart)

"SUPER SPITFIRE"
THE SPITFIRE F.21, F.22, AND F.24

The last operational versions of the Spitfire were originally intended to be named the "Victor," such were the differences between these marques and their predecessors. The first glimmerings of the new type began to appear in 1943 when the Griffon-powered Spitfire III development aircraft began test flying. The intended production version was originally designated the Mk.IV, although to reduce confusion with the rapidly expanding range of Spitfire variants, it was later redesignated the Mk.XX.

The second of these airframes, serialled DP851, first flew from the airfield at Worthy Down with a Griffon II engine in August 1942. Later that year the aircraft was re-engined with a R-R Griffon 61, resuming flight trials in December of that year. The resulting combination was then designated as an interim Mk.21.

Also replaced were the original wings which were superseded by a pair of similar planform, although these had a stronger, heavier gauge skin and revised internal structure. These also featured metal-covered ailerons capable of withstanding greater loads at higher speeds than the original fabric-covered items. This in turn required a redesign of the whole wing structure which began in 1942. All this was required to combat the possibility of aileron reversal which can be induced by the twisting of a lighter assembly.

Other changes incorporated in DP851 were centred on the fuselage, especially in the cockpit area where a new curved windscreen was installed as well as a canopy to match. At the rear of the airframe the aircraft was fitted with an original early-type fin matched to a broad chord rudder. Initial test flights were undertaken using a four-bladed propeller, although this was later changed to a five- blade unit.

LA215 was a Spitfire F.21 which spent most of its working life in the trials role engaged in Spiteful tail unit and contra-rotating propeller trials. (Eric B Morgan Collection)

This photograph depicts the first prototype Spitfire F.21, which was originally named the "Victor." Unlike the later versions of the second generation Griffon Spitfires, PP139 sports full-span wings. (C P Russell Smith Collection)

Flight testing of the Mk.20 revealed that the Spitfire had a top speed of 455 mph at 25,600 feet and a service ceiling of 42,800 feet. Measured climb rate was 4,800 feet per minute at a datum height of 7,700 feet. The flying life of DP851 came to an abrupt end in May 1943 when it was lost in a crash. Although the Mk.20 did not achieve production status, it did serve as the prototype for the succeeding Spitfire F.21. The first proper F.21 was PP139 which made its maiden flight on 24 July 1943 piloted by Chief Test Pilot Jeffrey Quill.

Externally the major difference between the "Super Spitfire" and its earlier Merlin- and Griffon-powered siblings was in the shape of the wings. These were completely redesigned and incorporated substantial strengthening to take advantage of the promised extra power available from the proposed Griffon series engines. Although the wing planform retained its basic elliptical shape, the trailing edge was straightened slightly which increased the wing's surface area, a much needed improvement for the higher altitudes required from this version.

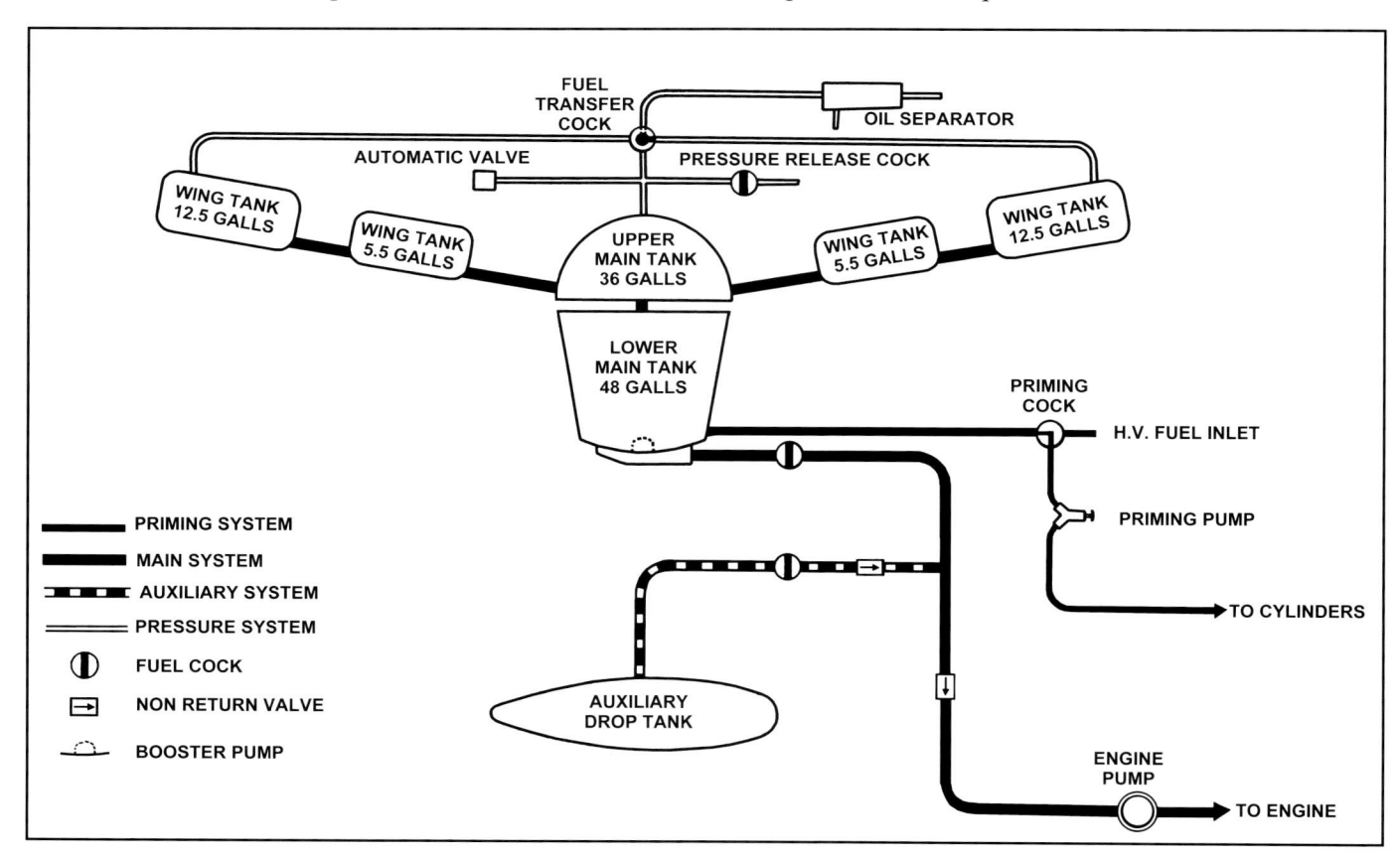

The fuel system installed within the Spitfire F.21 and later variants was far more complicated than that fitted to the first versions, therefore more care and management were required by the pilot. (Big Bird Aviation Collection)

Commensurate with the tweak to the wing's trailing edge came a significant change to the positioning of the ailerons which were moved slightly outboard and were some eight inches longer. Also altered was the method of mounting. Originally the greater majority of Spitfires used a pair of bearing mountings for each surface, whereas on the Mk.21 the mounting was via a continuous piano hinge which incorporated a balance tab for trimming and balance and improved the aircraft's rate of roll. On PP139 the wingtip assemblies were of the pointed variety although on production airframes they reverted to a blunter format.

Unlike previous Spitfires, the Mk.21 had only one wing-mounted armament option: four 20mm Hispano cannons with part of the belt feed system hidden under blister panels on each wing upper surface.

Other changes to the wing structure centred about the main undercarriage bays where an outboard fairing was provided for the main wheel which had previously remained uncovered on other marques. To ensure that the new doors did not foul the main wheel on retraction, a sequence valve was incorporated into the hydraulic operating system for each leg.

Although setting up and adjusting the various catches, rods, and locks was a complicated business, the addition of the wheel covers did result in a cleaner wing which in turn resulted in improved performance. However, the undercarriage bay dimensions remained the same in size, thus a complicated series of levers was used to compress the leg to allow retraction. A further change resulted in the undercarriage legs being lengthened and strengthened.

Spitfire LA232 wears the personal "TT" codes of AVM T C Trial although the aircraft was allocated to the HCCS. This particular aircraft was fitted with a contra-rotating propeller unit driven by a Griffon 85 engine. (C P Russell Smith Collection)

This in turn led to the tips of the propeller being raised higher above the ground. Stability in ground manoeuvring was also improved as the track of the undercarriage was increased from 5 feet 9 inches to 6 feet 8 inches.

The fuel system also underwent some changes with the addition of two small fuel tanks in the wing leading edge which added an extra 35 gallons of fuel to the usable total and brought the aircraft total up to 120 gallons.

The powerplant fitted to the Spitfire F.21 could either be the Griffon 61 or 64, both of which featured a slightly

Prior to its final use in the instructional role at RAF Cosford, Spitfire F.21, LA226, had seen use by No. 91 Sqdn and No. 3 CAACU at Exeter. Close study of the cannons will reveal that only blanking stubs remain. (C P Russell Smith Collection)

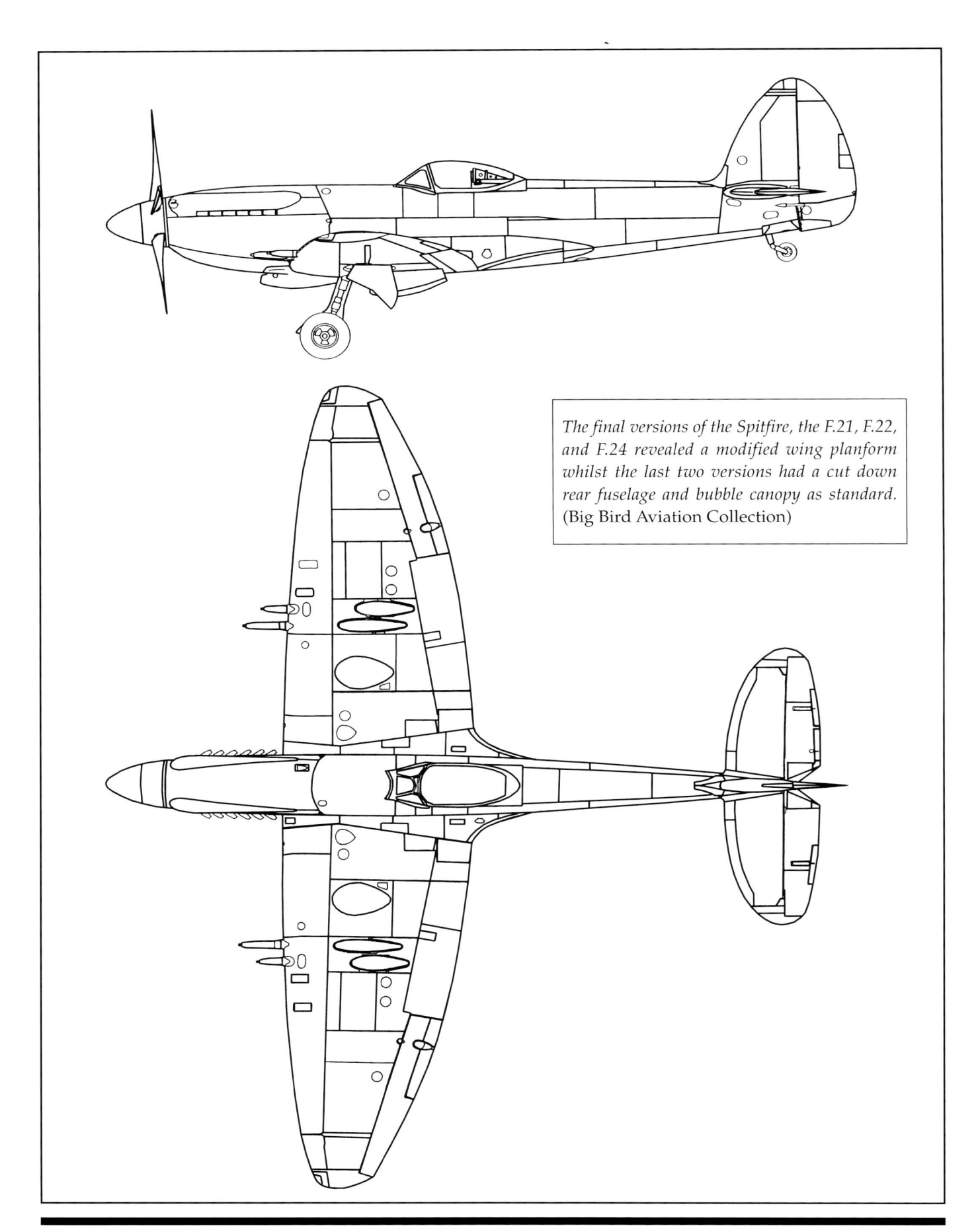

The final versions of the Spitfire, the F.21, F.22, and F.24 revealed a modified wing planform whilst the last two versions had a cut down rear fuselage and bubble canopy as standard. (Big Bird Aviation Collection)

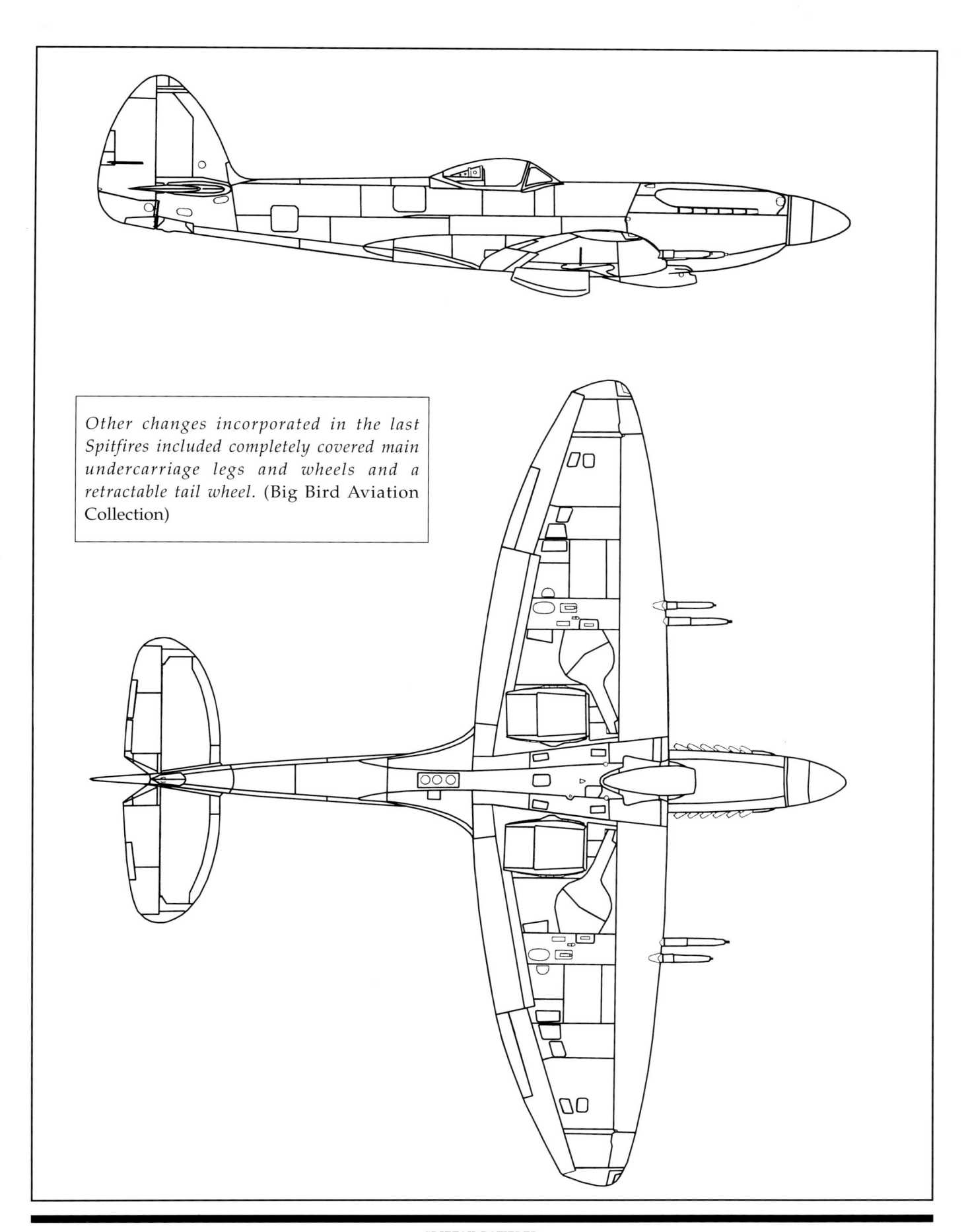

Other changes incorporated in the last Spitfires included completely covered main undercarriage legs and wheels and a retractable tail wheel. (Big Bird Aviation Collection)

different gear ratio from the Mk.XIV which had the Griffon 65 installed. At the receiving end of the engine's power output was a five-blade propeller similar to that fitted to the Mk.XIV series of airframes. The diameter was increased by seven inches to eleven feet. Another engine that featured in the F.21 was the Griffon 85 which was developed to drive a six-bladed contra-rotating propeller unit. The airframe used to trial this installation was LA218 which was dispatched to the AFDU at Tangmere in May 1945 for evaluation flying.

The report generated by these trials was very enthusiastic as the Spitfire had become a very stable gun platform due to the elimination of the effects of engine torque. These first examples of the contra-rotating propeller were occasionally unreliable although considering the amount of complicated engineering involved it was hardly surprising. Eventually, after many months of testing and development, the propeller unit became a tried and trusted piece of equipment although its only production usage was its installation in the Seafire FR.47. Engine cooling also underwent some changes as the oil cooler was moved to the starboard underwing position whilst the intercooler was placed in front of the radiator assembly under the port wing.

This first aircraft also had the windscreen and canopy design borrowed from the earlier DP851 whilst the fin had a straight leading edge and an enlarged rudder borrowed from the Mk.XIV although these were later replaced by units from the F.21 production line.

After PP139 came the first full production airframe, LA187, which undertook its maiden flight on 15 March 1944. This airframe retained the fully pointed wingtips of the earlier aircraft with the fin and rudder changed to that of the Mk.XIV. Also from the same source came the canopy and windscreen. However, these revisions actually resulted in an aircraft with performance levels that had deteriorated from the development airframes. This was officially reported after a series of

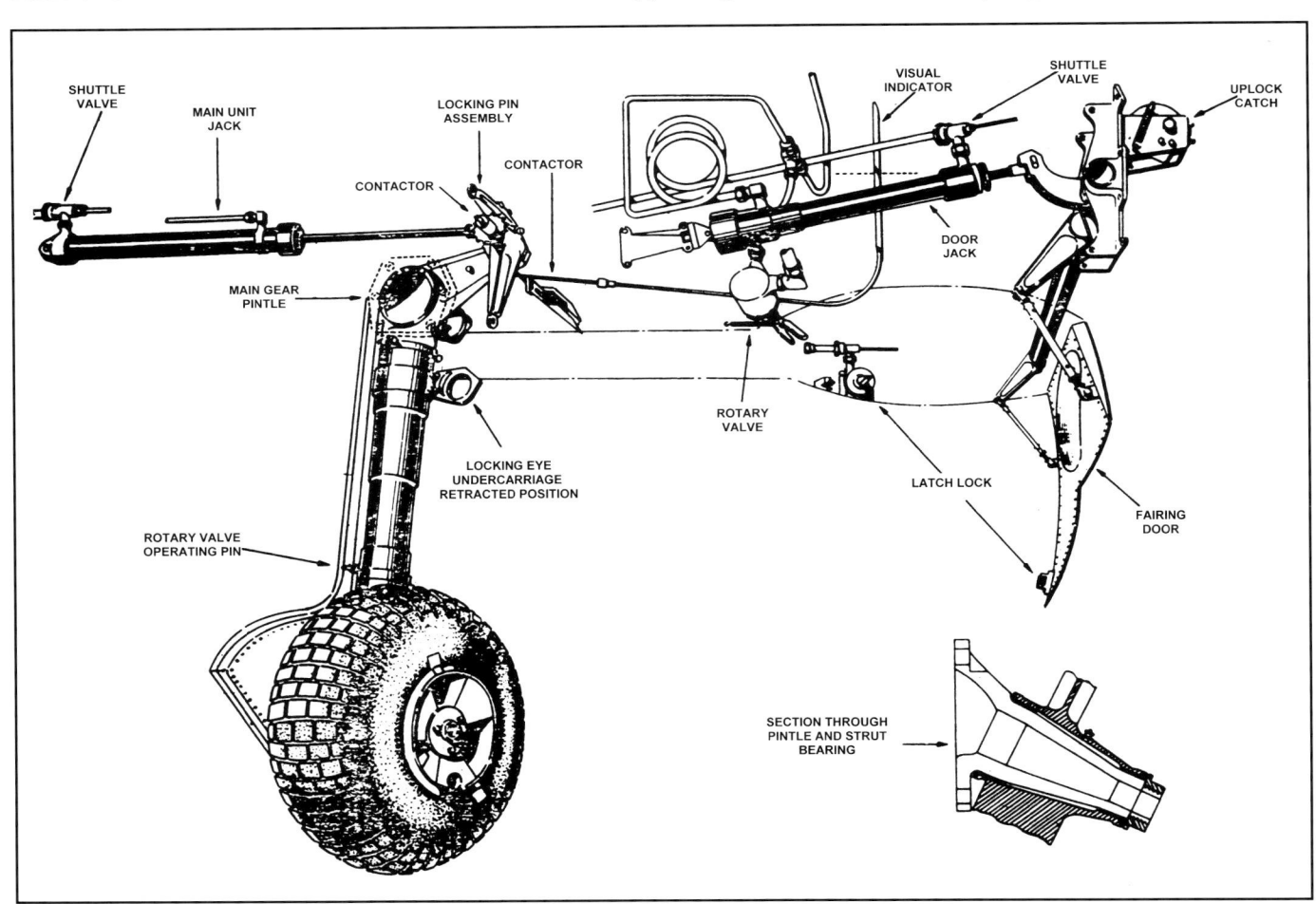

The main gear units of the later Spitfires and Seafires were wider in track and fully enclosed. (Big Bird Aviation Collection)

flight trials at Boscombe Down during November 1944.

The highlights included problems with rudder trimming, which was very sensitive and exacerbated by altitude. Further comments were applied to the general handling of the aircraft at its optimum operational height of 25,000 feet. Overall this report stated that the aircraft felt uncomfortable to handle during combat manoeuvres and had suffered a reduction in speed of approximately 15 to 20 mph.

Attention was paid to these reported faults. Therefore, when the fifteenth production aircraft, LA201, was sent to the AFDU at RAF Wittering for evaluation it was hoped that some improvement would be noticed. During these trials the top diving speed of 525 mph, improved rate of roll, and cannon armament were deemed worthy of praise. However, the final paragraph damned the Spitfire F.21 outright when it recommended that the type be withdrawn from frontline service and replaced by the earlier Mk.XIV. Although not dangerous, the aircraft was regarded as unstable for a gun platform.

This was not good news for both Fighter Command and Supermarine although the latter was aware that such a problem could occur. A fix was already in the process of being designed and involved the production of enlarged horizontal and vertical tail surfaces that would cure the over-control problem. Prior to the appearance of the modified rear section a series of experiments was undertaken to see if the problem could benefit from a temporary fix. This took the form of removing the rudder trim tab whilst the problem with elevators was cured by adjusting the trim tab gearing to half its range and replacing the original pointed horn balance tips with those of a more rounded shape.

Spitfire F.21, LA215, was the first production aircraft to feature all these changes and was dispatched to the AFDU, by this time incorporated into the Central Flying Establishment (CFE), once company flight testing was complete. The report from this unit praised the work that

Although F.21 LA198 was officially retired for gate guard duties when this photo was taken, it does reveal the more clipped wing fitted to production versions of the aircraft plus the outer fairing doors for the undercarriage units. (C P Russell Smith Collection)

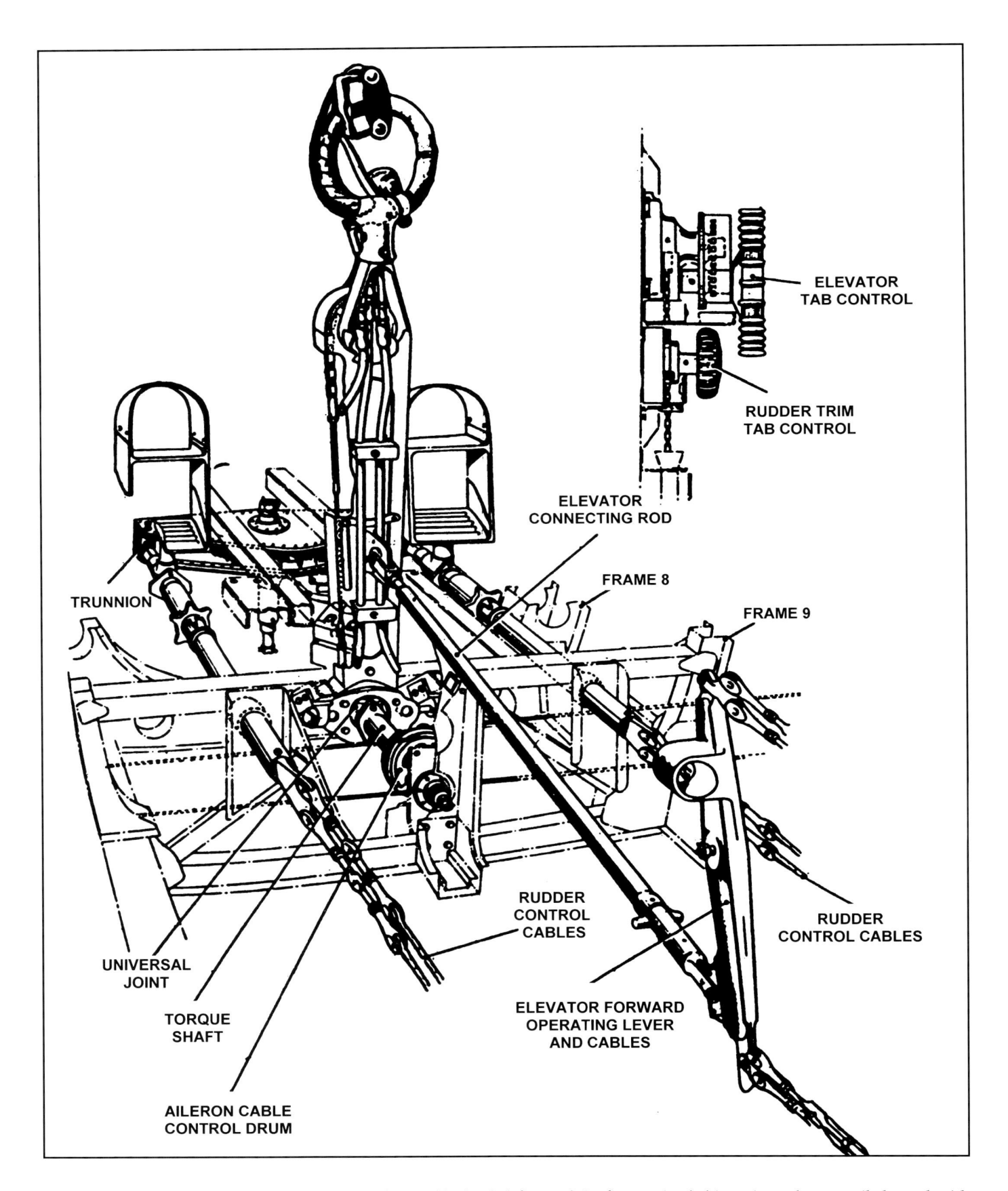

Possibly the most famous control column in the world, the Spitfire and Seafire retained this unique shape until the end with only minor changes. (Big Bird Aviation Collection)

Securely lashed down is this F.21, LA275, allocated to No. 602 Sqdn Royal Auxiliary Air Force. The bulged canopy is noticeable. (C P Russell Smith Collection)

Supermarine had carried out on the F.21 and went on to recommend that the aircraft at this modification state would be adequate for low-level and instrument flying. The report concluded that the Spitfire F.21 had several advantages over the Spitfire XIV: greater fire power; faster at all heights by some 10 to 12 mph; greater acceleration at the start of a dive; greater aileron control at speeds above 300 mph; and greater

Not a normal sight is a Spitfire under its protective covering, especially as the wartime aircraft were estimated to have an operational life of five hours on average. (C P Russell Smith Collection)

Spitfire F.22, PK312, was the first production aircraft and as such spent most of its life as a trials vehicle including trials of metal-covered elevators. (C P Russell Smith Collection)

range. Although there was still some problem with yaw at altitude at high speeds, the Spitfire F.21 could be considered a satisfactory aircraft for the average pilot.

The first frontline unit to receive the Spitfire F.21 was No. 91 Sqdn based at Manston. It accepted its first, albeit unmodified, aircraft in January 1945. These were replaced in March by a series of modified airframes, the originals having been returned to Supermarine for modification action before issue to another unit. Once the squadron workup had been achieved, No. 91 Sqdn and its 18 aircraft moved to Ludham in Norfolk to begin operations. These primarily concerned armed reconnaissance missions over the Hague where it was reported that the Germans were assembling V2 rockets.

As the war in Europe was running down, the production of the Spitfire F.21 was limited to only 120 examples. Other units that flew this marque of Spitfire included Nos. 1, 41, and 122 Sqdns although their tenure in frontline service had ended in April 1947 when No. 41 Sqdn relinquished its fighters. Although the main RAF units had disposed of the F.21, they still had a role to play in the inventories of the Royal Auxiliary Air Force Nos. 600, 602, and 615 Sqdns operated the type from 1947 until late 1950.

The development of the Spitfire not only involved that of powerplants, but also of the wing aerodynamics so that the best performance could be extracted from the overall design. First inklings of the perceived changes required to the aircraft were noted when a pair of Spitfire Mk.IXs were extensively tested to evaluate the behaviour of the wing at high Mach numbers. Aerodynamic behaviour of flying surfaces in the transonic region were well understood by Supermarine therefore they set about improving the design of the wing.

The original wing design placed the transonic centre of pressure just behind the leading edge. Therefore, a total revamp of the design was to place the centre of pressure closer to the centreline of the wing, thus creating a high-speed laminar flow design with a low drag coefficient. A further change saw the disappearance of the original elliptical wing which was replaced by a design with even degrees of taper to the front and rear edges. Overall this would have reduced the wing area to 210 square feet which was only a small reduction from the original 242 square feet of the longer span wings.

To actively test the reality behind the theory, a Spitfire Mk.VIII, JG204, was sent to the Royal Aeronautical Establishment (RAE) for experimental evaluation. The first changes involved resetting the wing leading edges to see how the aircraft would perform. This was followed by the fitment of new leading edges, although the change in the wing profile was not close enough to the intended design to prove it one way or the other.

Supermarine and other interested parties then decided that the only way to really test the laminar wing was to build an aircraft to fly evaluation trials. The original intention required the construction of an entirely new airframe. However, to cut costs and hasten the first flight it was decided to convert Spitfire F.21 prototype, PP139, to the new standard. This resulted in the aircraft being redesignated the F.23 and tentatively renamed the "Valiant." (Astute readers will note that the unused names for the two new versions of the Spitfire, Valiant and Victor, would eventually emerge as two of the jet-powered "V" bombers.)

On roll out the revamped PP139 exhibited some drastic changes from its previous existence. The wings were extended with very pointed tips which increased the span to 40 feet 6 inches whilst the armament of four cannons was retained, although plans had been laid to fit the production versions with six cannons. The fin, rudder, and tailplane were also changed, all were enlarged to improve stability. Although the converted Mk.VIII and PP139 continued to fly in support of the forthcoming Spiteful/Seafang development programme, the F.23 Valiant contract for 438 airframes was cancelled in early 1944 as nonviable and not required as the tide of war had turned in Europe.

Having departed down the F.23 development avenue, Supermarine returned to its original design path with a new version of the F.21 fighter. This was designated the F.22 and was built from the outset with a cut down rear fuselage and bubble canopy for improved pilot vision. The rest of the airframe was pure F.21 in execution.

This aircraft is the penultimate F.21 which served with No. 600 Sqdn Royal Auxiliary Air Force. The clearness of this shot shows the outer gear doors, cannons, and the rear view mirror above the windscreen frame. (C P Russell Smith Collection)

Another change concerned the electrical system which was upgraded from the original 12 volts to 24 volts, this feature first appearing in the later F.21 fighters. The first production F.22, PK312, was rolled out in March 1945. Initial test flights revealed similar handling characteristics to the previous F.21 and a few of its vices. After initial Supermarine test flights, PK312 was dispatched to A&AEE, Boscombe Down, for further testing and weighing where it was perceived as a vast improvement on earlier aircraft even though it was the heaviest Spitfire thus far. During this period the much promised enlarged tail surfaces were finally installed, which gave the F.22 an increased overall length of 31 feet 11 inches.

Further trials were carried out during 1947 using 500-pound bombs to extend the Spitfire's capabilities. AUW of the F.22 was averaged at 9,309 pounds, an increase of only four pounds over the F.21. The installation of the revised tail unit made an instant improvement on the handling of the Spitfire F.22 making it a far better gun platform. Use of the installed fuel tank in the rear fuselage still remained officially prohibited.

As the war in Europe ended there was very little need for the F.22, especially as the RAF was in the process of contracting to peacetime levels. Production orders were set at 260 airframes in total. Only one frontline unit, No. 73 Sqdn based in the Middle East in Ta Kali, Malta, would receive this new marque of Spitfire in July 1947. Its tenure in frontline service was short as No. 73 Sqdn traded in its aircraft for the DH Vampire jet fighter in October 1948.

Another handful of aircraft were used by the Flying Refresher Schools until 1951 when they began to enter long-term storage where they were to remain until declared obsolete in May 1955. During this nonflying period various storage methods, including humidity-controlled cocooning, were evaluated for future use. A final total of 278 Spitfire F.22s were built, most were to serve with the Royal Auxiliary Air Force until replaced by either the DH Vampire or the Gloster Meteor jet-powered fighters.

After withdrawal many of the redundant airframes were dispatched to various Maintenance

This slightly high-angle shot of Spitfire F.22, PK340, shows some of the normally hidden detail on the wing upper surface. This includes the fairings above the Hispano cannon breaches and that above the undercarriage wheels. (C P Russell Smith Collection)

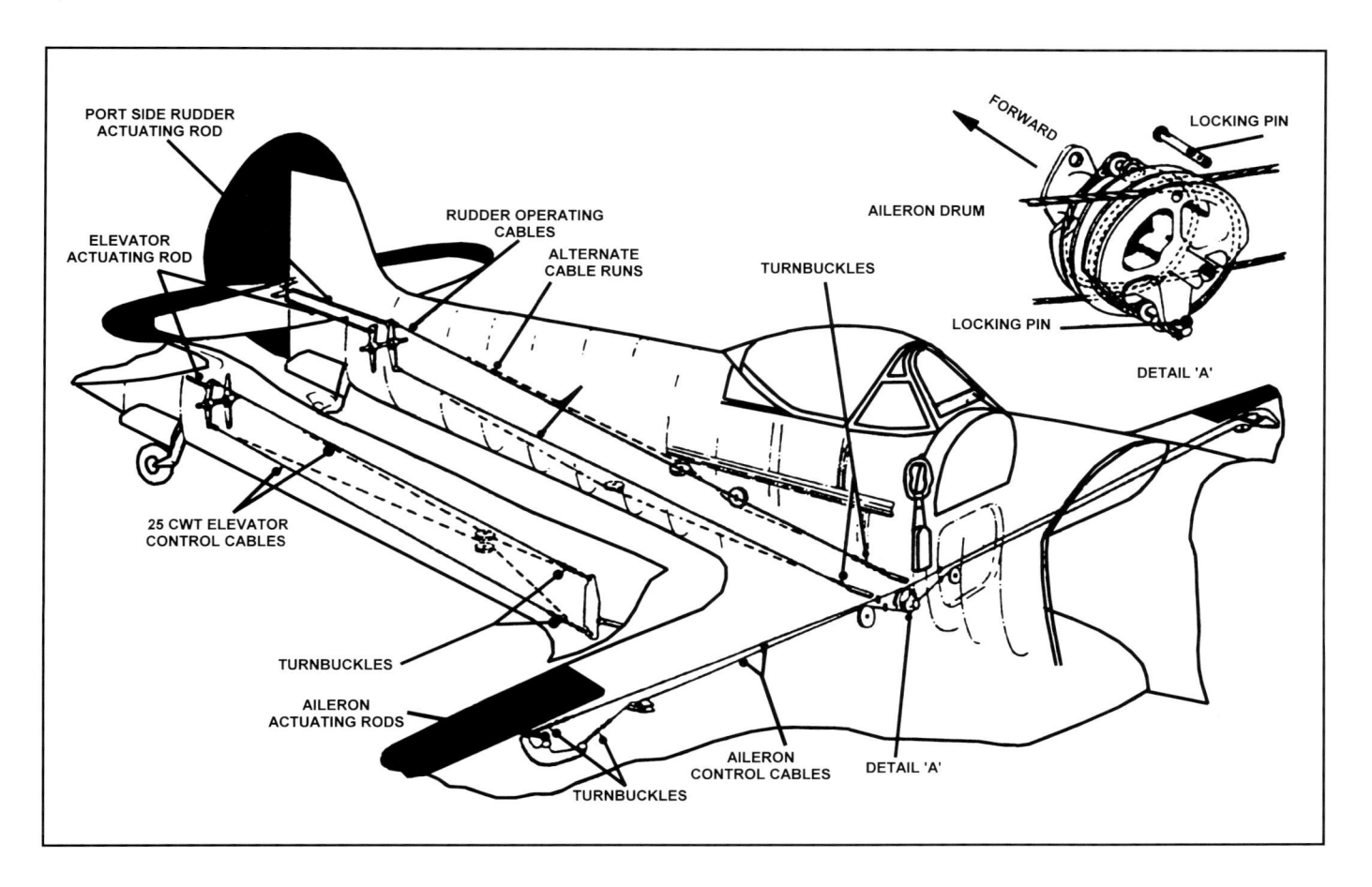

Although the last marques of this famous aircraft were built with the rear fuselage of the Spiteful, the control runs and their assembly still owed much to the prototype. (Big Bird Aviation Collection)

Units (MUs) to await their fate. Not all were scrapped, however, as 22 airframes were exported to the Southern Rhodesian Air Force, 20 went to the REAF, and 10 to the Syrian Air Force.

Externally the final version of the Spitfire produced by Supermarine for the RAF was the same as the preceding F.22. In fact, the changes introduced within the F.24 hardly justified the allocation of a new designation, these being a pair of 33-gallon fuel tanks in the rear fuselage. An extension to the weapons capability was added by the incorporation of underwing hardpoints for rocket projectiles. In the final batch of Spitfire F.24s the original long-barrel Hispano cannons were replaced by the shorter Mk.V version.

A total of 54 Spitfire F.24s were built by Supermarine, whilst a further 27 were obtained by converting some of the earlier F.22s. The first aircraft was released on 13 April 1946 whilst the last Spitfire delivered to the RAF, VN496, left the Vickers Supermarine works at South Marston on 20 February 1948. Only one operational RAF unit received the F.24, No. 80 Sqdn based originally at Gutersloh in Germany as part of No. 2 TAF.

During July 1949 the squadron decamped to the RAF base at Kia Tak, Hong Kong, to join the Far East Air Force (FEAF). The squadron's 18 aircraft were shipped to their new base on the aircraft carrier HMS *Ocean*. No. 80 Sqdn continued to operate the Spitfire F.24 until it was replaced by the twin engine DH Hornet fighter, a development of the earlier Mosquito. Instead of returning the unit's aircraft to the UK, most were handed over to the Hong Kong Auxiliary Air Force, which continued to operate them until they were retired in April 1956.

There was one attempt to sell the surplus aircraft to Argentina as part of a combined package with a batch of ex-RAF Lancaster bombers in the event only the bombers were purchased. Some of the unused Spitfires were used for storage trials alongside the earlier redundant F.22s using various forms of preservation. Some 20 airframes underwent this process which began in 1952 and was to end in 1956 when the aircraft were sold for scrap.

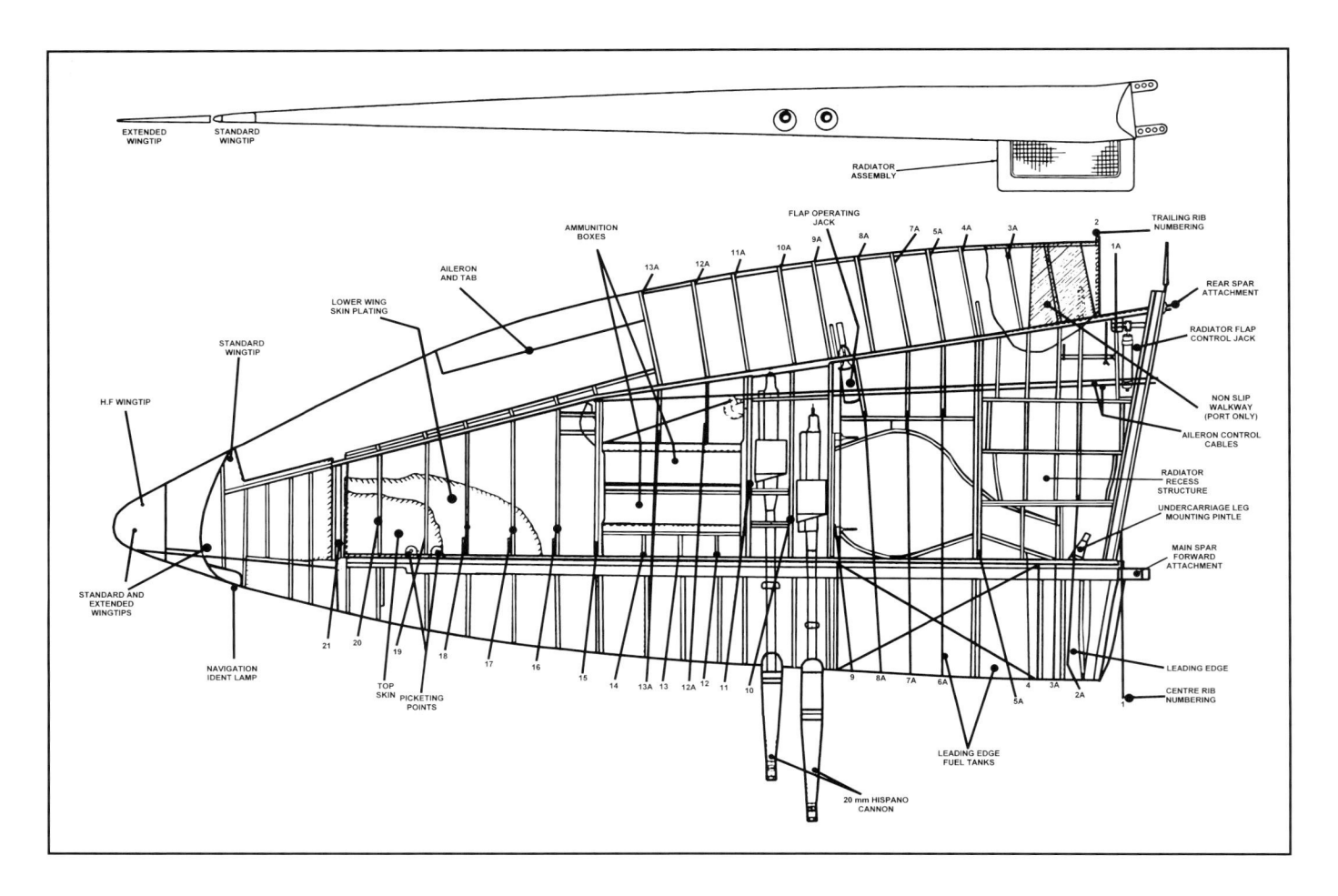

The wing structural assembly for those Spitfires in the final series was still based on that of the prototype although by the time the F.22/F.24 was achieved a great deal of strengthening had taken place. (Big Bird Aviation Collection)

Photographed in 1947, Spitfire F.22, PK657, is in immaculate condition. The subtle blending of the wing and fuselage is clearly evident. (C P Russell Smith Collection)

PK559 sports all the modifications applied to the type including the Spiteful tail assembly. (C P Russell Smith Collection)

Spitfire F.22, PK430, is also taking part in the Kings Cup Air Race. To enable the aircraft to perform to its maximum performance, the weapons and their ammunition were removed to reduce the all up weight. (C P Russell Smith Collection)

PK577 taxies out to begin its day's flying. Allocated to No. 607 Sqdn this particular airframe had a life of nine years before being scrapped.
(C P Russell Smith Collection)

This view of Spitfire F.22, PK346, of No. 613 Sqdn Royal Auxiliary Air Force shows quite clearly the Spiteful tail unit that was retrofitted to these early-built aircraft to cure a longitudinal instability problem. (C P Russell Smith Collection)

After its short frontline operational life was over, Spitfire F.22, PK497, spent some time at Old Sarum on gun firing trials. Unlike the early-built aircraft, this machine was constructed with a Spiteful tail unit.
(C P Russell Smith Collection)

After service with the Royal Air Force, some Spitfire F.22s were sold to other air forces. This aircraft, 681, was sold to the Egyptian Air Force. As the Spitfire was due to undertake a long delivery flight it is fitted with a centreline slipper tank. (Eric B Morgan)

This aircraft is shown in the parked position which entailed lashing the control column in place in the cockpit to stop the surfaces from moving. Although allocated to No. 603 Sqdn the markings indicate that it was taking part in the Kings Cup Air Race in 1950. (C P Russell Smith Collection)

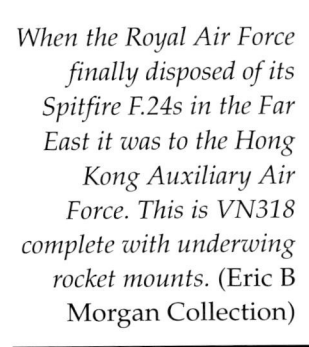

When the Royal Air Force finally disposed of its Spitfire F.24s in the Far East it was to the Hong Kong Auxiliary Air Force. This is VN318 complete with underwing rocket mounts. (Eric B Morgan Collection)

This might be the final pure version of the Spitfire built, but that famous top to the control column is still evident. (Chris Michell)

From a slightly different angle the whole of the pilot's panel is revealed as is the compass to the left of the control column. (Chris Michell)

This view of a Spitfire F.24 with the covers removed from the Griffon engine reveals the side bearer mounting beam and engine exhaust stubs. (Chris Michell)

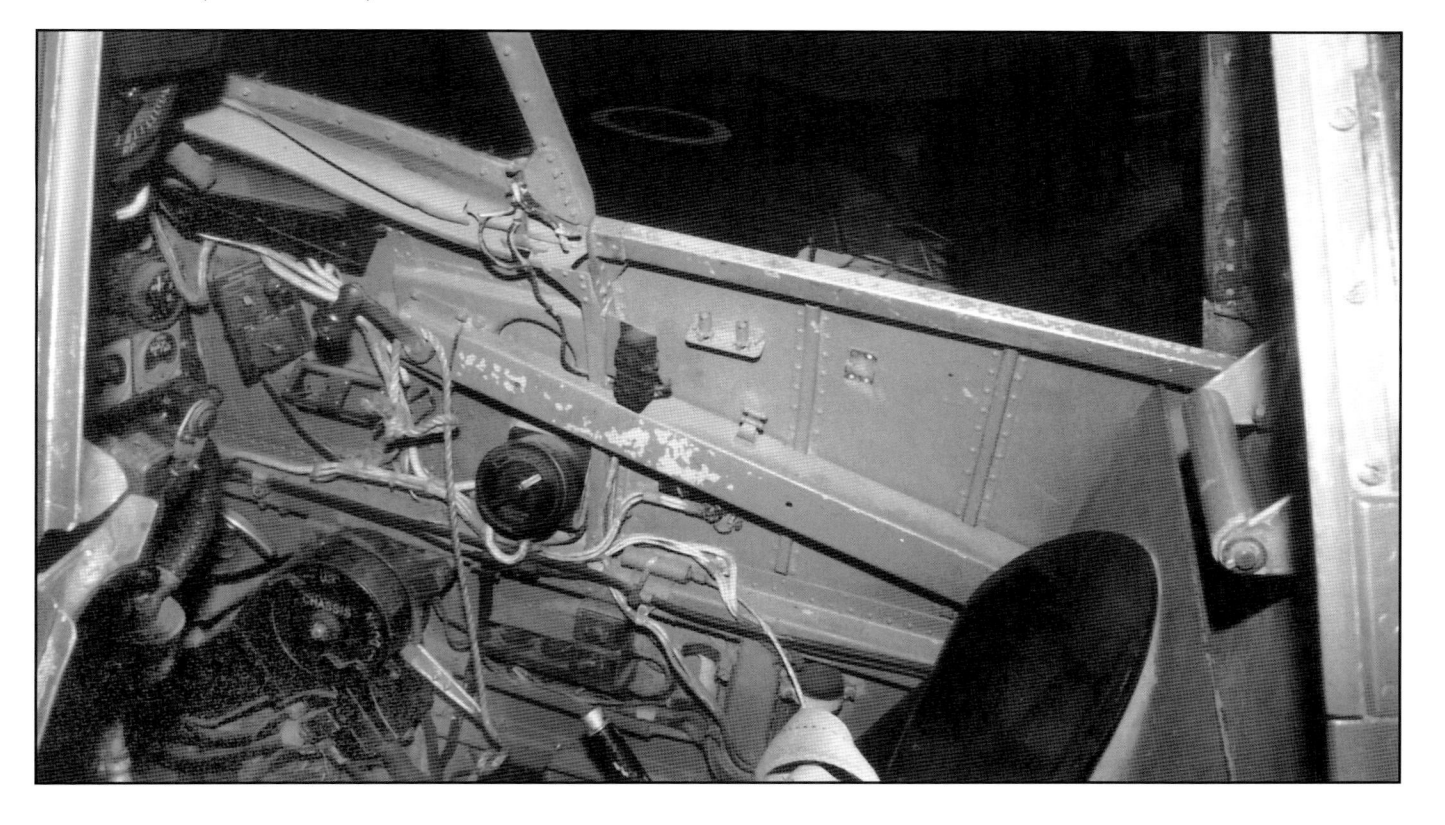

The right-hand cockpit wall plus its structure is evident in this shot of an F.24 cockpit as is part of the fixed windscreen frame. (Chris Michell)

PK713 was originally constructed as an F.22, but was later converted to F.24 standard. During its delivery flight the aircraft suffered the indignity of an undercarriage malfunction which made for a difficult landing. All the detail of the undercarriage and other systems is clearly revealed. (C P Russell Smith Collection)

This view of Spitfire PK683 clearly shows all the skin panel and access panel lines associated with the type. (C P Russell Smith Collection)

Combat Colours
Of the Spitfire and Seafire

By the time the Spitfire Mk.XII entered RAF service, the original colour scheme of green, dark earth, and duck egg blue had been replaced with colours more suitable for operations in more temperate climes. This consisted of dark green overlain on medium sea grey in a disruptive pattern with undersurfaces in a lighter shade of grey. Some duck egg blue remained, however, in the form of a tail band whilst the leading edges were given a thin yellow stripe. This stripe helped differentiate the type from the aircraft of the Luftwaffe to anti-aircraft gunners although some reports stated that such a recognition feature was almost impossible to see against the sky.

When the F.XIV and the F.XVIII joined the inventory they too were camouflaged in a similar manner to the earlier F.XII. Some alterations to the finish were inevitable when some of these machines were deployed to the Far East. On some aircraft the grey was replaced with dark earth whilst all had South East Asian Command roundels, with the red centre removed, applied to all six positions. The tail flash also lost its red stripe and all aircraft in theatre were given wide white stripes above and below the wing and on the rear fuselage. After the cessation of hostilities, most aircraft had their camouflage removed and flew in a natural metal finish, with national markings to suit, until withdrawal.

When the reconnaissance version of the Griffon Spitfire, the PR.XIX, entered the inventory of the Royal Air Force, it was given an overall Photo Reconnaissance Unit blue finish. Few alterations were made to this scheme. One main change was the application of light grey to the upper fuselage of those airframes based in the Far East as part of Far East Air Force. Only one other PR.XIX changed its finish, PS888, which was operated for a while in an unpainted state.

Of the final Griffon-powered Spitfires, the F.21 flew on operational sorties in the European temperate scheme although some were to lose their camouflage after the

Spitfire F.XIV, RM689, was once operated by Rolls Royce. Here it sports authentic markings applicable to a European-based aircraft except for the Rolls Royce flash on the cowling. (C P Russell Smith Collection)

war ended. Of the F.22, those few that actually enjoyed a period of active service wore the standard temperate finish. Those of No. 73 Sqdn were bedecked with the unit's flashes on the fuselage side. When the Spitfire F.22s were transferred to the Royal Auxiliary Air Force, the greater majority flew in an unpainted state with peacetime roundels and fin flashes applied. Unit markings were in the form of coloured bars on each side of the fuselage roundels. The last Spitfire type built for the Royal Air Force, the F.24, was originally delivered in the standard temperate scheme although this soon gave way to the normal peacetime unpainted finish.

Those aircraft sold or diverted to overseas customers were frequently transferred in the finish initially applied, thus the PR.XIXs of the Swedish Air Force were only renumbered and remarked with Royal Swedish Air Force marks before delivery. Others, such as those aircraft sold to Burma and Thailand, were delivered in an unpainted state with only national markings to brighten the airframe.

The aircraft delivered to the Fleet Air Arm followed the needs of wartime, thus the Seafire Mk.XVs operating in the Far East wore a two-tone finish on their upper surfaces with sky undersurfaces. As they flew in the South East Asian Command theatre of operations, the relevant markings minus the red centres and bars were applied. Those Seafires in service in more temperate climates normally wore dark sea grey uppersurfaces with sky underneath offset by standard roundels and fin flashes.

This trend continued after hostilities ended. Therefore the Seafire Mk.XVIIs, F.45s, F.46s, and FR.47s retained the full depth dark grey upper surfaces until a change in policy saw the extension of the original sky undersurface colour farther up the fuselage and over the fin and rudder. By this time the fin flash had disappeared, being replaced by a two-letter unit/ship code. The roundels on the wings also assumed equal proportions for all three colours. Seafires also wore invasion stripes both over the D-Day landings period and later when the FR.47s of No. 800 Sqdn were involved in combat operations over the Korean theatre of operations.

Wearing the standard Photo Reconnaissance Unit blue finish topped off by South East Asian Command markings is PR.19, PM631, which had previously seen service with THUM flight prior to retirement. This Spitfire is currently flown by the BBMF from RAF Coningsby. (Nick Challoner)

Seen in the Battle of Britain hangar at RAF Coningsby is Spitfire PR.19 PS915 with its undercarriage raised whilst being supported by jacks and trestles. Note the counter balance weight hanging from the rear fuselage.
(C P Russell Smith Collection)

This photograph of MV293 reveals an aircraft in the immediate postwar scheme of overall silver. This particular airframe was operated for a period by the Indian Air Force before returning to the UK and adopting No. II Sqdn markings. (Nick Challoner)

The markings worn by PS915 are those of No. 152nd Sqdn when it was based in the Far East Air Force during 1946. (Nick Challoner)

This Spitfire FR.XVIII, SM845, had a very short Royal Air Force career before moving on to the Indian Air Force. After retirement the aircraft was purchased for private use. (Sander Wittenaar)

Still wearing its Hong Kong Auxiliary Air Force markings is Spitfire F.24, VN485, which had originally been preserved at Kai Tak. (Nick Challoner)

Seen in front of a retired Phantom is Spitfire F.22, PK624, when it was in store at RAF Abingdon. The Phantom was subsequently scrapped whilst the Spitfire is still extant. (Big Bird Aviation Collection)

RM689 is a Spitfire F.XIV which wears the unit markings of No. 350th (Belgian) Sqdn when it was part of No. 2 Tactical Air Force in 1944. Unfortunately, this Spitfire was badly damaged in a crash landing. (Big Bird Aviation Collection)

Captured in storage at St. Athan, this Spitfire F.22 betrays its last role as a gate guard by the inclusion of blanking plates in the radiators and the capping of the cannon barrels. (Big Bird Aviation Collection)

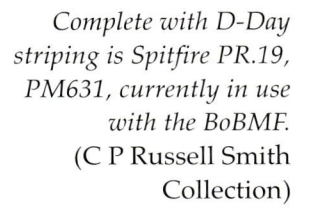

Complete with D-Day striping is Spitfire PR.19, PM631, currently in use with the BoBMF. (C P Russell Smith Collection)

Spitfire PR.19, PS853, achieved a measure of fame whilst based with the BBMF at RAF Binbrook where it was used in tactical trials for the resident Lightning fighters. It still flies with the BBMF and currently wears the standard temperate Photo Reconnaissance Unit blue markings complete with D-Day invasion stripes. (Big Bird Aviation Collection)

This close up (right) of the starboard main gear clearly shows the anti-drag links behind the main wheel and the tie down points facing the camera. (Big Bird Aviation Collection)

Above: *To the rear of the main gear bays are the wing-mounted radiators complete with filter grilles. These are standard on all the Griffon-powered Spitfires from the F.XIV onward. (Big Bird Aviation Collection)*

Seen from a rear point of view this shot of a PR.19 reveals the Lobelle hood fitted over the cockpit and the relaxed state of the flying controls. (Big Bird Aviation Collection)

This view of a Spitfire FR.XIV clearly shows the enlarged tail surfaces required to counteract the torque of the far more powerful Griffon engine. The clipped wings, introduced to reduce wing panel stress, are evident in this shot. (Danny Jacquemin)

Preparing for takeoff is Spitfire PR.19 PS915 resplendent in South East Asian Command markings. Of note are the open radiator cooling flaps under the wing. (Nick Challoner)

SPITFIRES AT SEA

THE GRIFFON SEAFIRES

In the late 1930s the Royal Navy was reasonably well equipped with modern aircraft carriers, although the aircraft carried were mainly biplanes such as the Fairey Flycatcher and the Hawker Nimrod. The outbreak of hostilities in 1939 saw the FAA receiving its first monoplane fighter, the Fairey Fulmar. Although modern in outline, the aircraft was grossly underpowered and underarmed in comparison with its German opposition.

To compound the difficulties facing those charged with defending the ships of the fleet and the convoys bringing in vital supplies to Britain there was a distinct lack of carriers to cover these vital duties. Part of the answer came in the shape of Catapult Armed Merchantman (CAM) ships complete with one-time-only use Hawker Hurricane fighters which were used to defend the convoys. This, of course, meant that the aircraft was lost at the end of its sortie while the pilot, a precious asset, had his life placed in danger whilst awaiting rescue from the sea.

As the war progressed, more capital aircraft carriers and escort carriers were constructed to improve defences. These in turn required fighter aircraft capable of not only protecting the ships the carriers were escorting, but also capable of offensive operations against attacking forces and in support of ground forces. The first aircraft to undertake this role was the aforementioned Fairey Fulmar which was later replaced by the far more capable Fairey Firefly. This was a multi-person, multi-role fighter which found its niche in the long-range fleet defence role.

For the close fleet support role the Merlin-powered Seafire was found to be the ideal solution although this sea-going derivative of the Spitfire was at a slight disadvantage due to the narrow track of its undercarriage. These first versions of the Seafire, totalling three in number, added improvement upon improvement prior to the emergence of the Griffon-powered versions.

The Seafire XV was the first Griffon-engined version of the aircraft accepted by the Fleet Air Arm. This particular aircraft, SR583, was assigned to No. 767 Training Squadron. The two cannons sported by the Seafire are in fact dummy installations. (C P Russell Smith Collection)

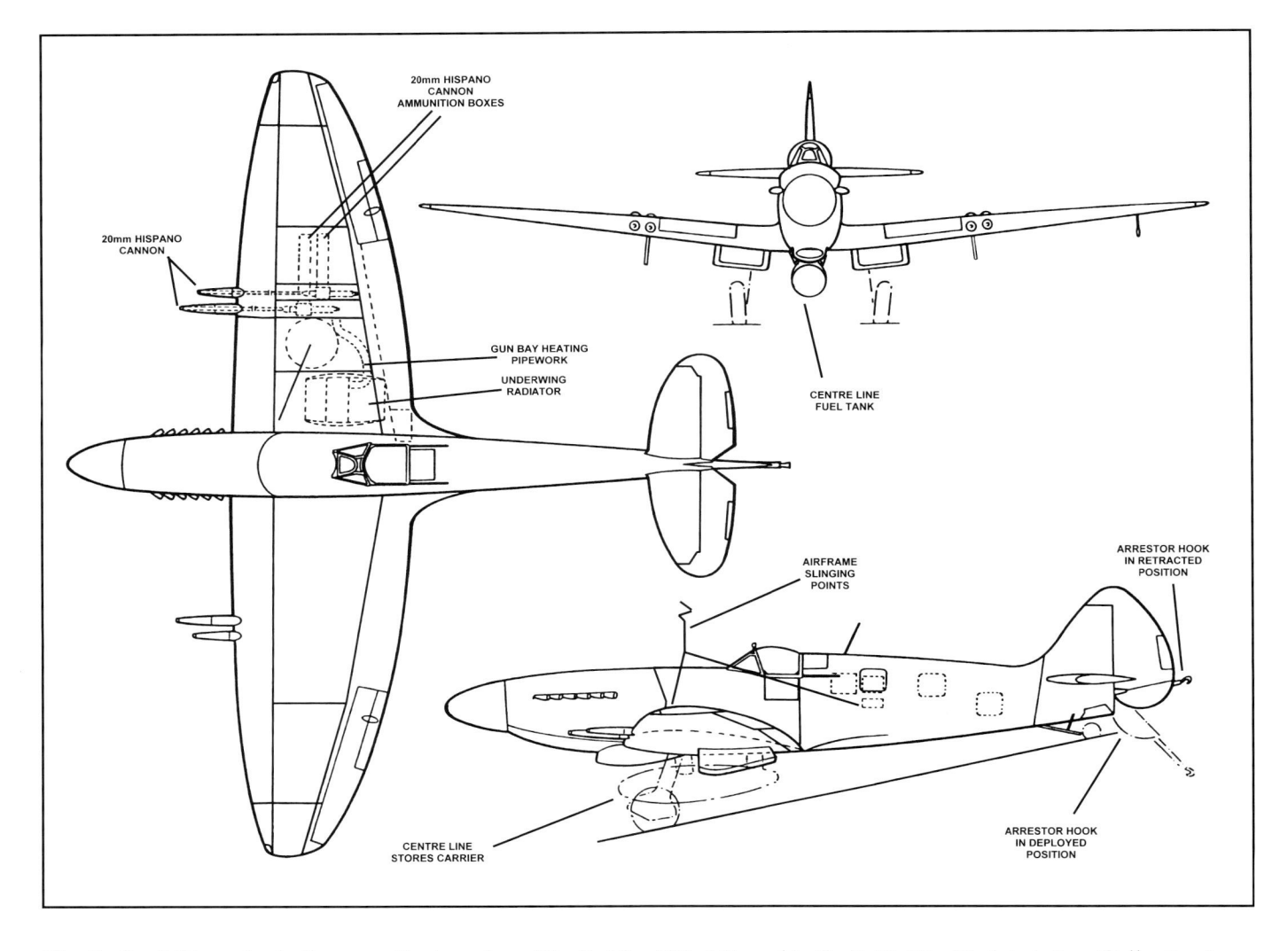

The Seafire F.45 was basically a navalised version of the Spitfire F.21 delivered to the RAF. (Big Bird Aviation Collection)

The first Seafires, a corruption of the name "Sea Spitfire," followed very closely their land borne counterparts, thus the appearance of the Seafire III was allied to that of the Spitfire Mk.V. Many would assume that the next marque for the Admiralty would therefore be based on the following Spitfire Mk.VIII or Mk.IX. However, the Air Ministry was reluctant to release these airframes as the former variant was required for service in the Far East whilst the latter airframes were needed for the UK-based squadrons. The Air Ministry did, however, suggest that some of the Spitfire Mk.VIIIs could be modified at a later date for carrier use.

Obviously this was unacceptable to the Admiralty, and it was decided to pursue a conversion of the first Griffon-powered Spitfire — the Mk.XII. In response, Supermarine issued a company specification to cover the new aircraft. This was an amalgam of many of the previous airframes although the basis was the Mk.XII. The engine installation was from that aircraft although the powerplant was the Griffon Mk.VI which drove a four-bladed propeller unit with a cooling system derived from that of the Spitfire Mk.V. This in itself was further updated by the use of an Mk.IX radiator. Internal fuel in Mk.IX fuel cells was set at 100 gallons with an external tank containing 60 gallons.

The fuselage was based on the Seafire Mk.III with the wings coming from the same source complete with folding mechanism which enabled each mainplane to compact into three parts with fold lines at the wingtip and just outboard of the main gear bays. The rear end was modified from the Mk.VIII complete with a broad chord rudder and retractable tail wheel.

Armament was based on the basic "B" type wing of the Spitfire Mk.V and consisted of a pair of 20mm Hispano cannons plus four .303 Browning machine guns. Externally, the Seafire was able to carry one 500-pound GP bomb on the centreline with fitments available for four external rocket projectiles. This marque of Seafire was also capable of carrying a pair of 250-pound bombs on underwing pylons.

With the requirements defined, the Admiralty issued Specification No. 4/43 for six prototypes with the Supermarine type number 377. Originally it was intended to designate the new fighter the Seafire XII although this was soon changed to the Mk.XV so that the habit of designations clashing and causing confusion was soon obviated.

The first production airframe was rolled out in November 1943 and was the beginning of a production run that covered 503 machines constructed by Westland Aircraft and the Cunliffe Owen organisation. These airframes were intended for production between July 1943 and March 1944 and were to differ from the prototypes in that the oil cooler was increased in size to match that of the engine radiator. Two other changes were a slightly longer engine cowling and a spinner of an increased size.

Not long after entering service the Seafires were forbidden to carry out deck landings due to a problem with the supercharger clutch slipping at high revolutions. By early 1947, however, the fault had been rectified by Rolls Royce which was supplying modified clutches to replace the defective items.

Delays to setting up the production lines meant that the first aircraft did not appear until late in 1944. Of the ordered total, 384 were fitted with an "A" frame arrestor hook originally seen on the Seafire III although it was upgraded to accept a loading level of 10,500 pounds instead of the earlier 7,000 pounds. From airframe 385 the "A" frame was replaced by a sting-type hook which was anchored to the rear fuselage stern post and incorporated part of the rear fuselage in the moving portion. When the hook was released for a carrier landing it was spring loaded into the down position extending as it did so.

To prevent bounce back on touchdown the hook was held in position by an oleo pneumatic damper. This did not prevent the hook from utilising the built-in lateral play available to catch the wire. Although the sting hook was a far neater installation than the earlier "A" frame, its location aft of the tail wheel led to some problems with it becoming tangled with the arrestor wire. To combat

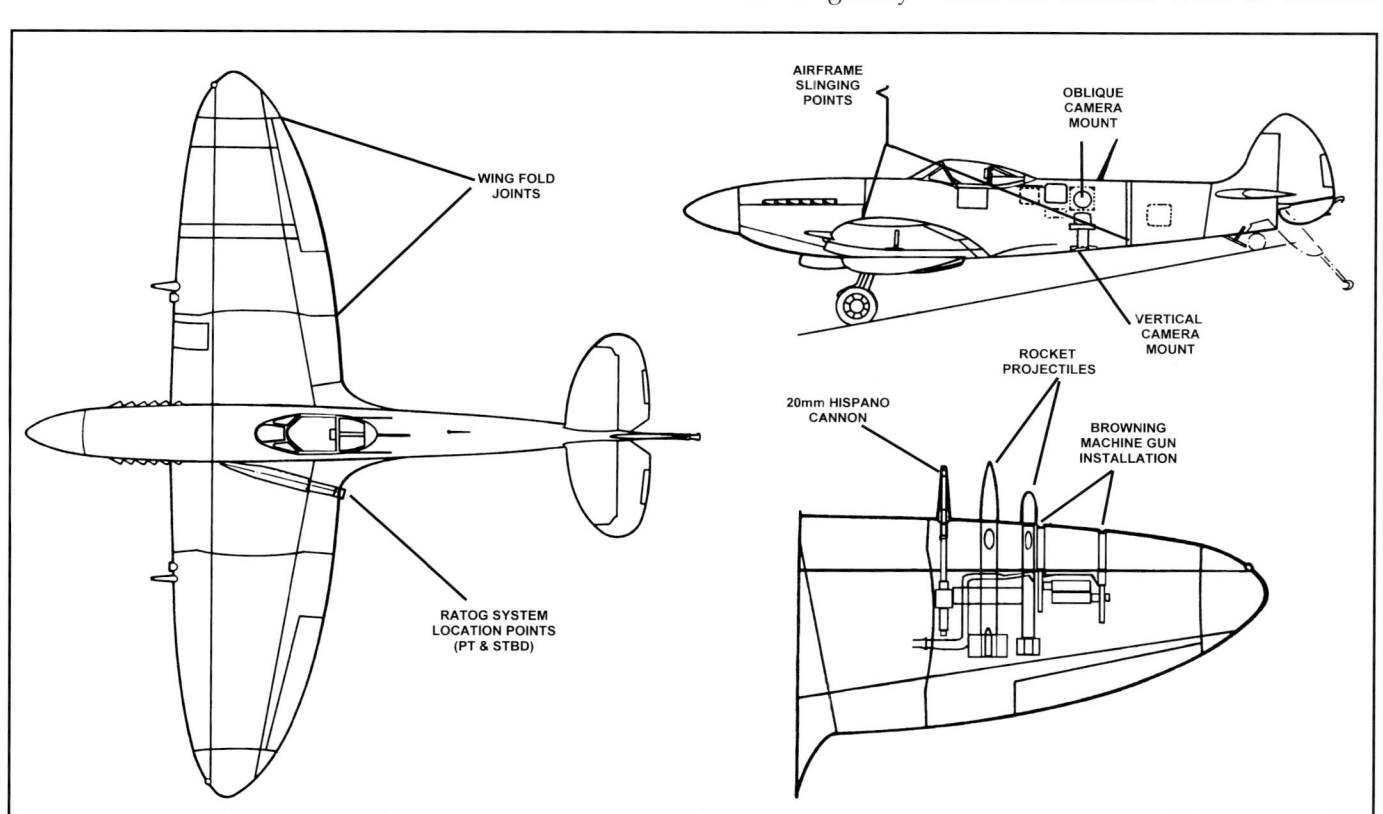

This general arrangement drawing of the Seafire FR.47 reveals the layout of the fuselage camera installation plus a selection of wing weapon loads. (Big Bird Aviation Collection)

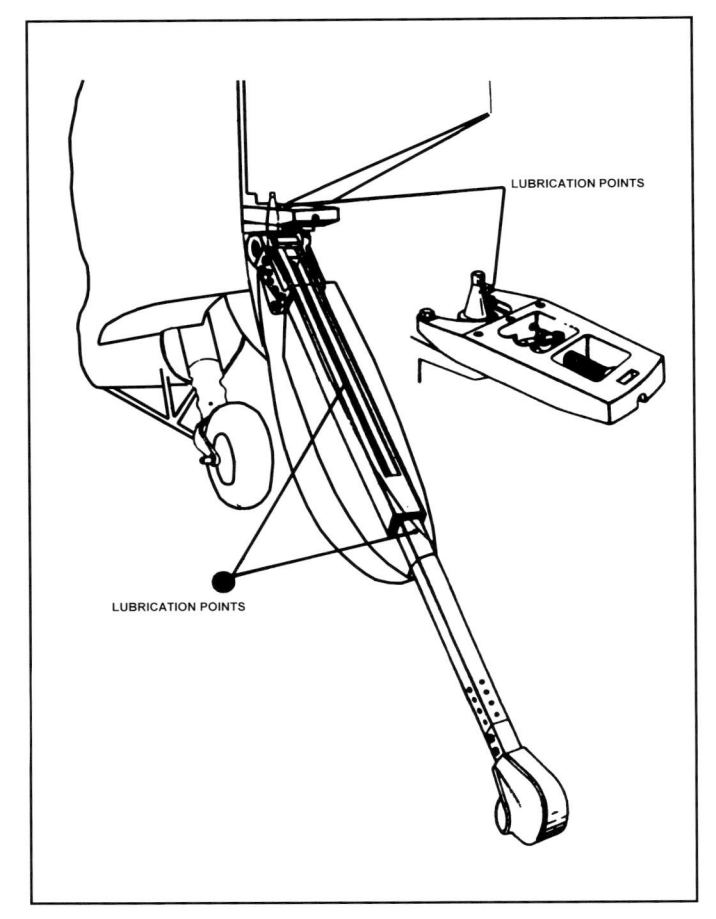

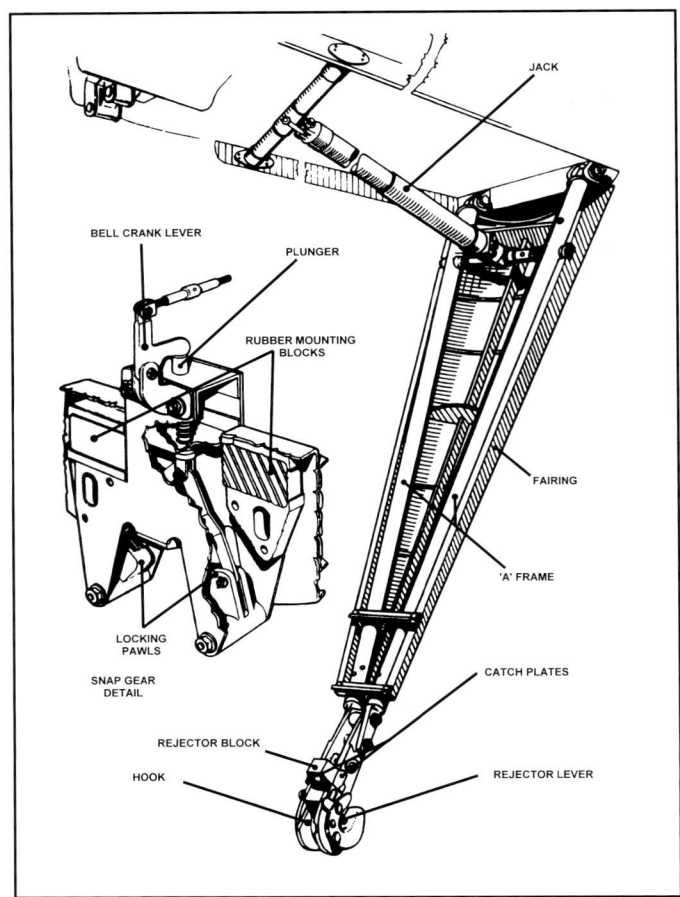

With the introduction of the Griffon-powered Seafire the arrester system changed from the earlier "A" Frame type to the sting hook type anchored to the rear fuselage fin post. (Eric B Morgan Collection)

Many pilots preferred the earlier "A" Frame installation which appeared to retard the aircraft quicker and drew on the greater strengths of the aircraft's structure at that point. (Eric B Morgan Collection)

this, a guard was installed in front of the tail wheel to deflect the wire onto the extended hook.

In contrast, the primary method of despatching aircraft from an aircraft carrier was originally a straight unassisted takeoff under the aircraft's own power. This was later supplemented by steam catapults located on the carrier's bow. The FAA was also aware that there might be occasions when the Seafires might need launching from less than ideal decks. In order to boost the liftoff characteristics of the aircraft the Royal Navy required that they be fitted with RATOG as well as the obligatory catapult launch spools.

It was also suggested that an improved method of launching be developed to improve takeoff speeds after catapult acceleration.

Theory suggested that a tail down attitude would improve the presentation of the wing leading edge to the airflow, therefore a Seafire F.XV was put forward for testing. The initial rear tie down points were found rather weak although the situation was much improved after strengthening was carried out. Also modified were the main undercarriage legs which would allow the airframe to absorb stress loads up to 2.25 Gs. Further trials involving the RAE and Supermarine revealed that under most conditions the Seafires performed admirably.

The first unit to equip with the Seafire Mk.XV was No. 802 Sqdn in May 1945 followed by Nos. 800, 803, 804, 805, and 806 Sqdns. As the Seafire Mk.XV was withdrawn from frontline usage it passed to the Royal Naval Volunteer Reserve (RNVR) squadrons whilst others were passed onto the Royal Canadian Navy which received 35 aircraft. Only two foreign sales were made. The first sale in late 1945 was to the Union of Burma Air Force which received 20 de-navalised aircraft and the second sale was to the French Navy which was to operate

15 aircraft from 1948. Only one other moved outside the control of the FAA when an Mk.XV in a high-gloss silver finish and completely stripped of armour plate was leant to the U.S. Navy Test Centre for handling evaluation.

The version of the Seafire that was to follow from the Mk.XV was the last of the old-type versions which was designated F/FR.17 depending on its role. The airframe used in the development of this new version was an Mk.XV, NS493, which was delivered to Westland Aircraft for conversion. Intended as a naval equivalent in standard to its RAF counterparts, the airframe underwent a reduction in the depth of the rear fuselage so that a bubble canopy driven by a manual hand crank could be fitted. In order to provide a means of escape during the takeoff and landing process the aircraft was flown with the canopy fully wound to the rear. To ensure that the hood would not spring forward during a normal or emergency landing the cockpit entrance door was locked in the outer catch position thus acting as a brake.

In common with most aircraft built or converted to this configuration the reduction in fuselage side area led to longitudinal stability problems, especially when the rear fuselage fuel tanks were filled. To alleviate this problem in the F.17, an enlarged rudder was fitted which helped to reduce the instability. Other changes from the earlier F.XV included strengthened wing and fuselage structures plus improved oleo legs for the main undercarriage. Other modifications included installation mounts plus ports for a pair of F.24 cameras in the rear fuselage just aft of the cockpit.

Fuel capacity for this version was 145 gallons housed in two tanks in the fuselage plus two in the wings. As the Spitfire and the Seafire had developed so the fuel system had become more complicated, therefore careful management was required to maintain stability otherwise control of the aircraft would become difficult. So that the rear fuselage fuel tank could be filled, operating procedures were put in place that allowed it to be used by the pilot on takeoff. It remained usable until it was empty. However, this was only

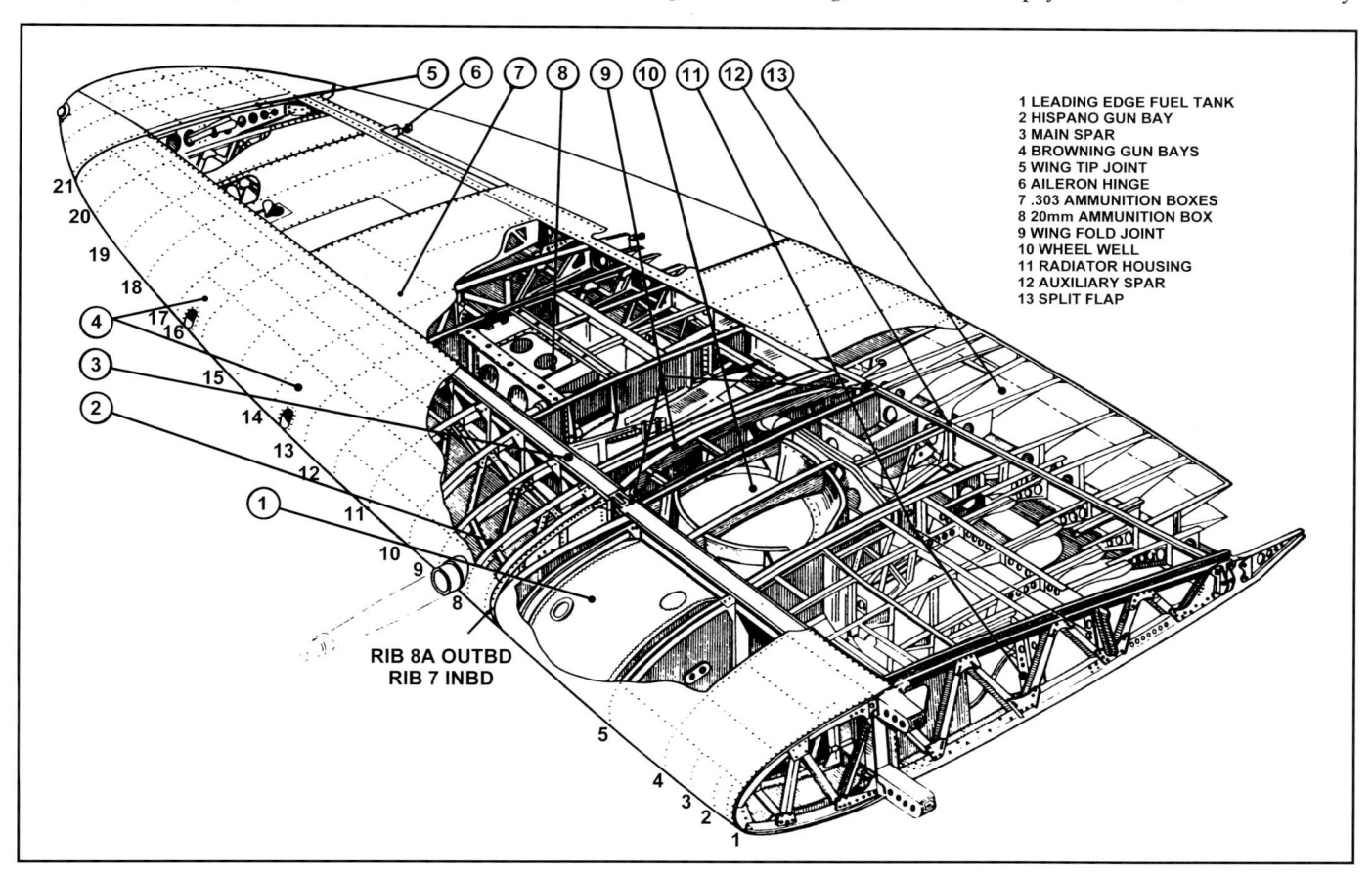

1 LEADING EDGE FUEL TANK
2 HISPANO GUN BAY
3 MAIN SPAR
4 BROWNING GUN BAYS
5 WING TIP JOINT
6 AILERON HINGE
7 .303 AMMUNITION BOXES
8 20mm AMMUNITION BOX
9 WING FOLD JOINT
10 WHEEL WELL
11 RADIATOR HOUSING
12 AUXILIARY SPAR
13 SPLIT FLAP

The wing structure of the later versions of Seafire were all similar in their form of construction except that the FR.47 featured a wing fold mechanism. (Eric B Morgan Collection)

After a very short service career, Seafire F.XV, PR433, was used as a training airframe. Here the airframe is mounted on servicing jacks awaiting its next batch of trainee engineers. Of note is the folded-down wingtip.
(C P Russell Smith Collection)

possible if the aircraft was flown gently as violent direction changes made the Seafire very unstable. In order that the maximum distance could be flown on missions, plumbing was provided for the carriage of external combat fuel tanks.

The powerplant fitted to the F.17 was the Griffon Mk.VI which drove a four-bladed wooden Rotol constant-speed propeller unit which rotated in the opposite direction to that of the Merlin, initially confusing some pilots. Such was the torque generated by this combination that the rudder trim had to be fully deflected in the opposite direction during takeoff to maintain directional control.

Armament was a pair of Mk.V Hispano cannons with 60 rounds per gun plus four Browning machine guns with 350 rounds per gun in a universal wing. External armament included one 500-pound bomb or a pair of 250-pound bombs, alternatively eight 60-pound rockets and their mounts could be fitted to the outer wing panel installation points. All this was toted on an airframe which had a wingspan of 36 feet 10 inches and a length of 31 feet 10 inches which later changed to 32 feet 3 inches when the enlarged rudder was installed. Weight when empty was 6,300 pounds which increased to

After the hostilities in Europe ceased, excess airframes were despatched to various allies. One of those that received the Seafire was the RCN for operational use from the aircraft carrier HMCS Bonaventure. This is one of the earlier batch of F.XVs built with the original underfuselage "A" frame hook. (C P Russell Smith Collection)

Another redundant Seafire F.XV that joined the RCN was this late-production aircraft complete with sting tailhook and guard for the tail wheel.
(C P Russell Smith Collection)

This manufacturer's photograph of a Seafire F.XV reveals many of the differences between this and its land borne counterpart. The Griffon Spitfires were built with five-bladed propellers whilst those machines for the Fleet Air Arm were equipped with a four-bladed unit. In common with all naval aircraft, the Seafire has an arrester hook located under the fuselage.
(C P Russell Smith Collection)

a normal load of 8,000 pounds although this could be extended to a maximum of 9,100 pounds. Maximum speed of the F.XV was 392 mph at 36,000 feet. The F.17 could manage the same sort of performance. Both had a service ceiling at the 37,000 foot mark whilst the range of both sat between 376 and 903 miles depending on the fuel load.

Production versions of the F/FR.17 began to appear in late 1945 with deliveries to No. 883rd Sqdn beginning in September. Total production, after the cutbacks of cancelled contracts, was to stabilise at 212 by Westlands and another 20 from Cunliffe Owen. Other frontline units to equip with the F.17 included Nos. 800, 803, 805, and 807 Sqdns. When these aircraft departed from the frontline inventory they were passed onto the RNVR and training units. These variants of the first generation Griffon Seafires were to finally disappear in November 1954.

The second generation Griffon Seafires for the Fleet Air Arm closely paralleled the development of their RAF counterparts. Thus when the RAF ordered the Spitfire F.21 in

Parked in storage at Royal Naval Air Station Stretton is Seafire F.XVII, SX358, awaiting its fate. Of note is the way the wing sections fold.
(C P Russell Smith Collection)

The Seafire F.XVII was very much a development of the earlier F.XV, the primary differences being a cut down rear fuselage and bubble canopy. This aircraft is SX156 of No. 767 Sqdn and is parked awaiting its next sortie. The open cockpit access door is worthy of note as are the angles assumed by the flight control surfaces in the restrained position. (C P Russell Smith Collection)

Seafire F.XVII, SP343, was allocated to Royal Naval Air Station Culham when pictured in 1949. Unusual for a postwar Seafire in the training role, the aircraft sports a centreline fuel tank. (C P Russell Smith Collection)

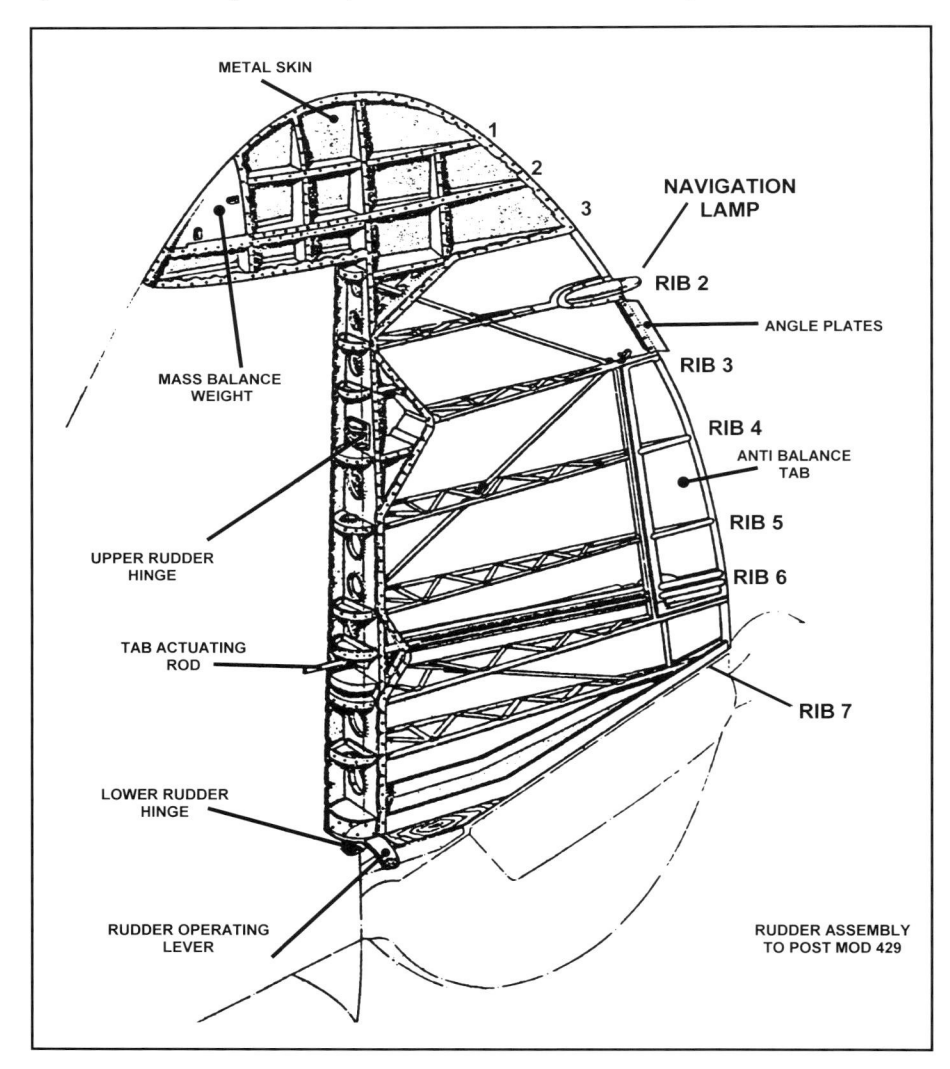

When the Seafire was fitted with a sting hook the surface area of the rudder was increased. (Eric B Morgan Collection)

large quantities the Admiralty looked to converting the design for naval use. To cover production of the aircraft for Fleet Air Arm use the Admiralty issued Specification N.5/43 to authorise the production of the F.21 as the Seafire F.45.

The firm Cunliffe Owen was the organisation selected to build the prototype under license although it was intended from the outset that the F.45 would act as an interim lead-in aircraft for those to follow. Therefore, to allow production to proceed quickly, minimal changes were authorised from the original Spitfire, thus such naval features as wing folding were missing.

The prototype was a converted F.21, TM379, which was fitted with slinging points, a naval VHF radio setup, and a sting-type arrestor hook. Other changes from the land-based aircraft were alterations to the main undercarriage fairings. Those attached to the legs were shortened to clear the arrestor wires whilst the outer bay doors were increased in size.

Soon after roll out and initial manufacturer's flight testing the aircraft was delivered to the Supermarine test airfield at High Post for initial weighing. By November 1944 the prototype was undergoing carrier landing trials aboard the HMS *Pretoria Castle*. During these trials the aircraft was affected by the torque generated by the Griffon engine which had a tendency to cause the aircraft to crab sideways on approach. This tendency notwithstanding, the F.45 was faster than earlier aircraft and had a faster rate of roll.

In an effort to reduce the crabbing tendency, TM379 was fitted with a contra-rotating propeller unit. To drive both sets of propellers the origi-

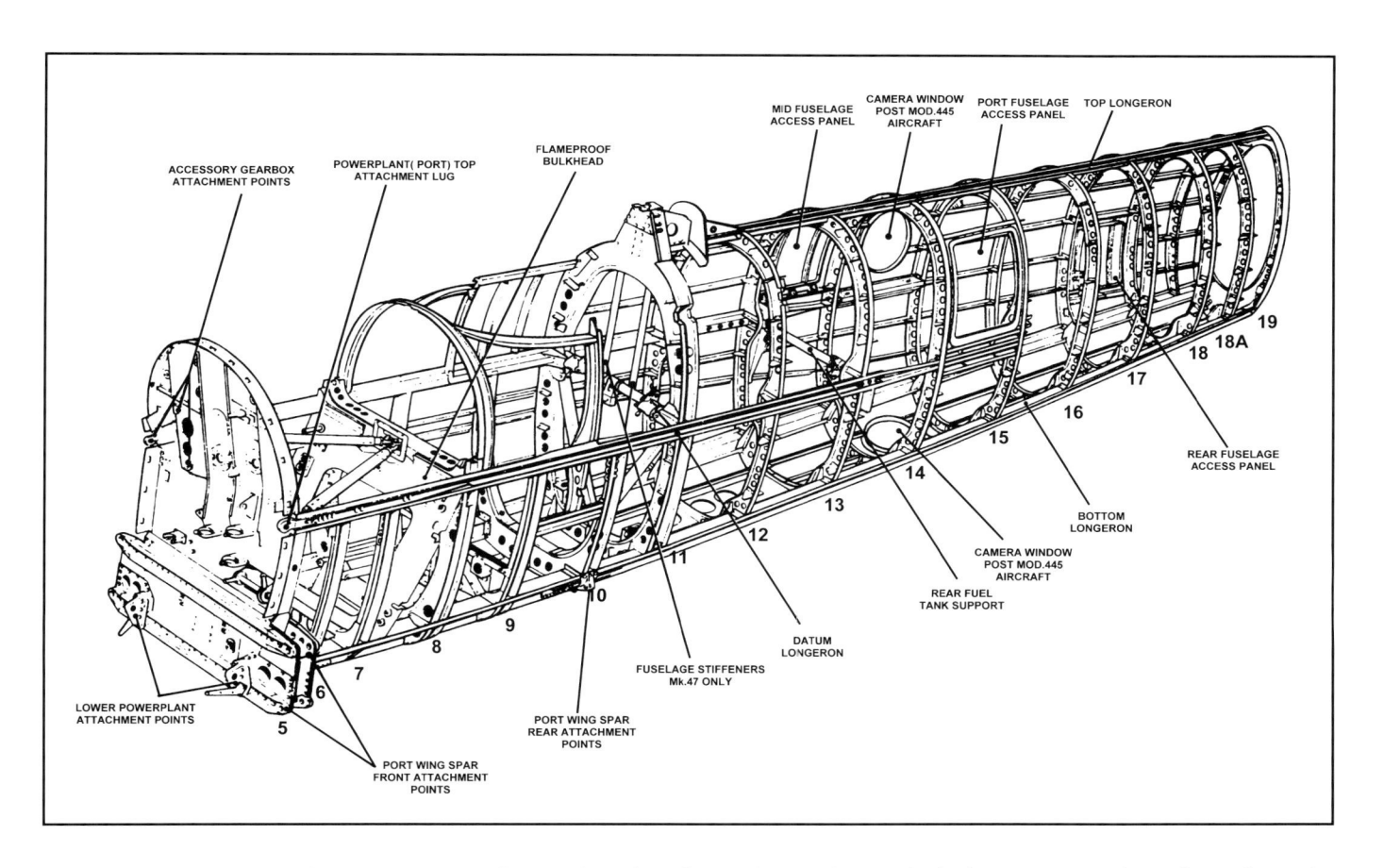

From Frame 5 aft to the fin post, most Spitfires and Seafires featured a similar method of construction throughout the entire range. (Eric B Morgan Collection)

nal Griffon 61 was replaced by the Griffon 85 which was more suited for this role. During carrier and general flight trials the F.45 was far more stable during takeoff and landing and, when properly trimmed, the Seafire was an excellent performer.

Seen as a taster of the aircraft to come, Seafire F.45 production at Castle Bromwich was limited to 50 examples, none of which would see frontline service. In November 1946 some of the F.45s entered the inventory of No. 778 Sqdn where they were used as conversion and lead-in trainers for the later-built F.46/F.47 Seafires. After withdrawal from flying duties a few of the redundant aircraft were used for crash barrier trials in connection with the forthcoming Westland Wyvern strike fighter.

The next sequential Seafire to follow was the F.46 which essentially was a semi-navalised version of the Spitfire F.22. In common with the aforementioned Spitfire, the F.46 shared the cutdown rear fuselage and bubble canopy although the installed powerplant was the Griffon 87 which in turn drove a six-bladed Rotol contra-rotating propeller unit. In order to maintain stability this variant was manufactured from the outset with the enlarged Spiteful tail surfaces, the broad chord rudder and fin assembly proving especially beneficial. As before, the main form of retardation was a sting-type arrestor hook for which a guard was installed in front of the tail wheel to stop entanglement with the arrestor wires.

Further takeoff assistance was provided by the installation of catapult launch spools and wing root reinforcement for the mounting of RATOG equipment. Armament was standard with the F.22 Spitfire although the wings were strengthened to carry rocket projectiles and the usual assortment of bombs and fuel tanks.

One primary feature omitted from the Seafire F.46 was that of wing folding which precluded its use aboard aircraft carriers with the FAA's frontline units. Very much an interim aircraft, only 24 airframes were constructed, the first making its maiden flight in September 1944. During its service life the F.46 was flown by Nos. 736, 738, 767, 771, 777, 778, 781, and 787 Sqdns in a training role although the odd specimen was operated by the various trials organisations. One such speci-

This shot of a Seafire FR.47 on a test flight clearly reveals the camera port in the upper fuselage, the wing cannon armament, and the underwing fuel tanks specific to the second generation Seafires. (Fleet Air Arm Museum)

men was LA544, employed on anti-spin trials during 1946 for which it had an anti-spin parachute and fin guard fitted. Just prior to leaving the service of the FAA, the remaining Seafire F.46s were operated by No. 1832 RNVR Sqdn.

The final definitive version of the Seafire to see FAA service was the FR.47 which was a fitting finale to the Spitfire line begun so many years before. At first glance the FR.47 looked little different from the preceding F.46. However, under the skin it was a much improved machine and was the only Griffon-powered version from the second generation to feature folding wings. In the first four airframes these were manually powered although this subsequently changed to a fully hydraulic system.

The first prototype development airframe, PS944, was manufactured as a pure fighter earning the designation F.47. After initial company test flights and evaluations by the various test organisations, the production line began to deliver the definitive FR.47 which included standard mounts in the rear fuselage to mount cameras in the vertical and oblique positions.

Further changes from the F.46 included a rear fuselage tank capable of containing 32 gallons of fuel. Other changes saw the engine carburetor intake extended to sit fully underneath the engine cowlings. To improve performance, the Griffon 88

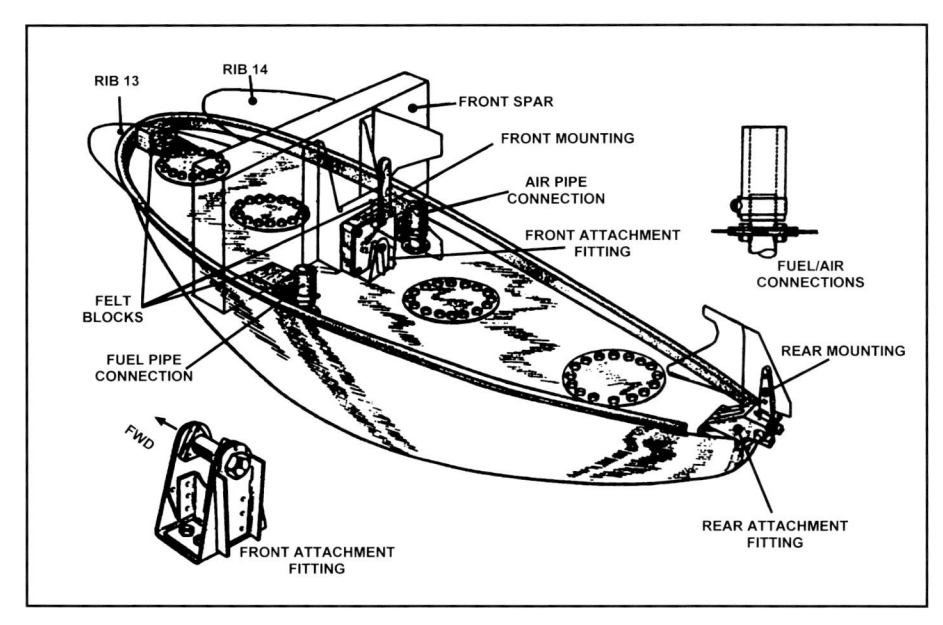

The Seafire FR.47 was fitted with underwing combat tanks more conformal in shape than the normal drop tanks. (Eric B Morgan Collection)

The final evolution of the Seafire was the FR.47. This version introduced all the navalisations required for carrier operations. Although the only frontline operator was No. 800 Sqdn, some did see use by the second line and reserve units. It is to one of the latter that VP455 is allocated, in this case No. 1833 Sqdn. (C P Russell Smith Collection)

engine was given fuel injection and drove a Rotol contra-rotating propeller assembly. Another improvement incorporated to improve takeoff and landing performance was an increase in the flap area by 20 percent plus the installation of longer stroke main undercarriage legs which were of the nonrebound variety, being more than capable of absorbing the increased operating weights possible with the FR.47.

To evaluate the new fighter, No. 778 (Trials) Sqdn was formed at Royal Naval Air Station (RNAS) Ford in December 1946 with some of the first aircraft to leave the production line. This small unit carried out deck landing and takeoff trials aboard the carrier HMS *Illustrious* during May 1947. A further evaluation unit, No. 787 Sqdn, was formed at West Raynham in 1947 to act as the types tactical development unit.

Although the development and tactical trials were pushed through quickly it was all for naught as hostilities ceased in Europe and the Far East. The urgency for the deployment of the FR.47 eased so deliveries and creation of frontline squadrons slowed. Thus it took until January 1948 for the first unit to form for car-

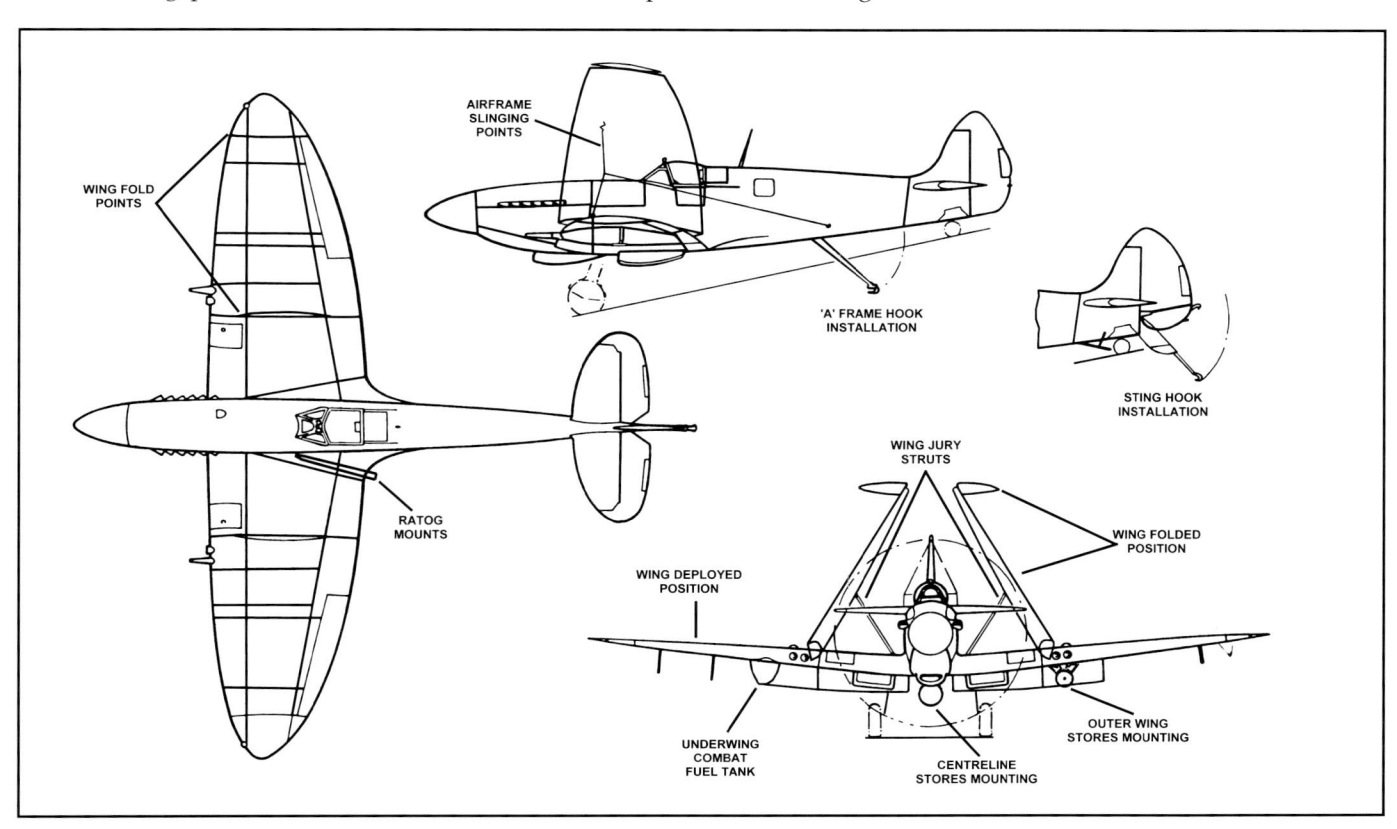

This general arrangement drawing illustrates both the Seafire F.XV and Seafire F.XVII. (Big Bird Aviation Collection)

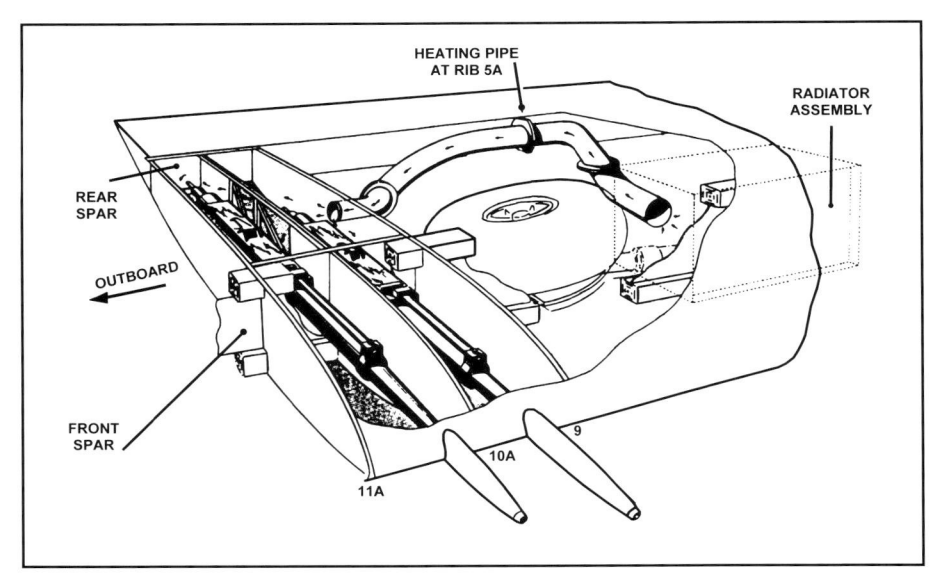

The wing guns in both the Spitfire and Seafire required heating to ensure their efficiency at increasing altitudes. (Eric B Morgan Collection)

rier duties, this was No. 804 Sqdn which later undertook sea trials and a deployment aboard HMS *Ocean* and later HMS *Triumph*. The last Seafire FR.47 delivery, of the 90 ordered, was in January 1949 when VR791 was flown out of the Vickers Supermarine manufacturing plant at South Marston.

In April 1949, No. 800 Sqdn became the second of the FAA's frontline units to receive the FR.47. This situation existed for only four months as No. 804 Sqdn re-equipped with the Hawker Sea Fury. Initially, No. 800 Sqdn was based at RNAS Sembawang on Singapore Island where the new aircraft was used in support

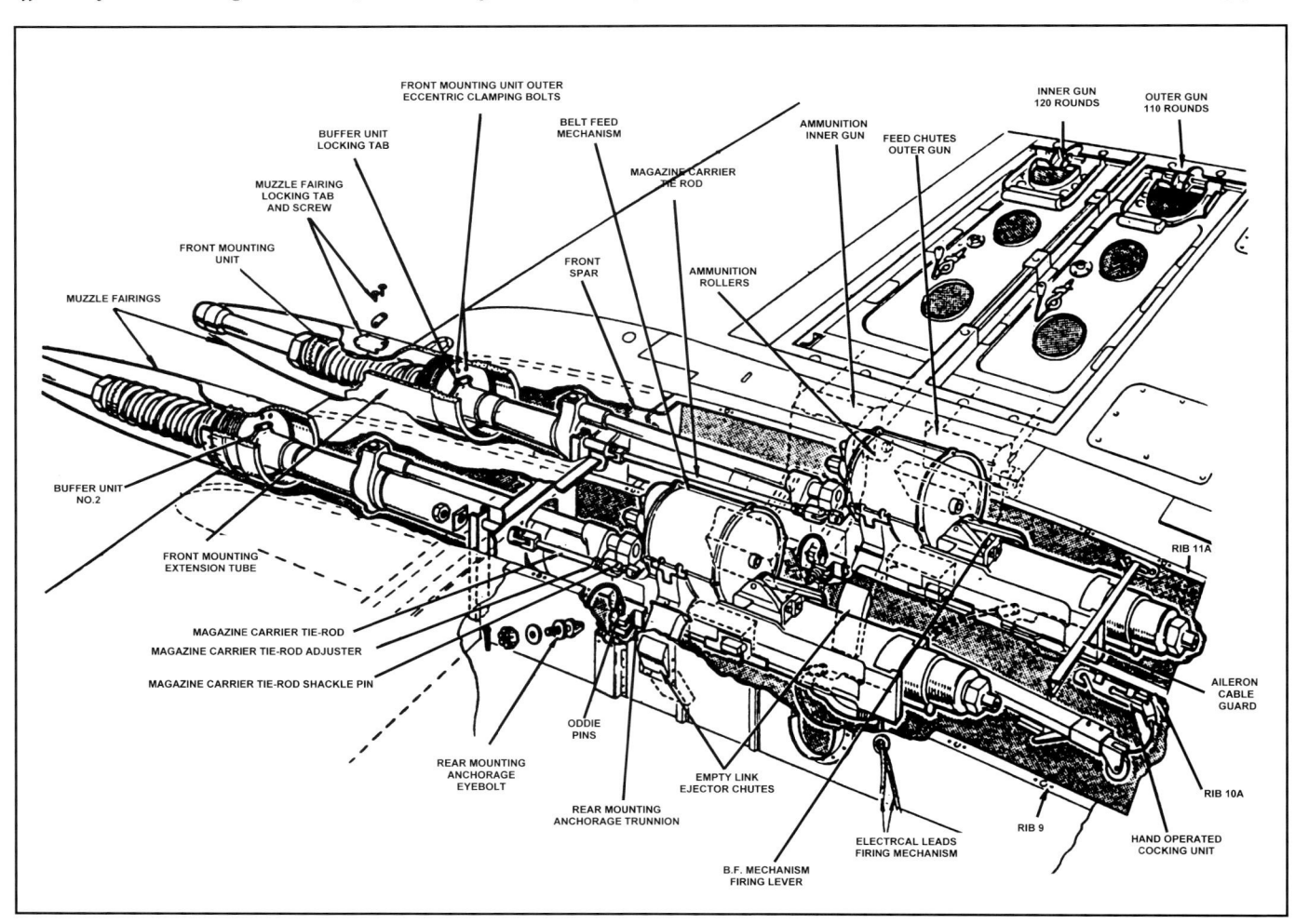

The Hispano cannon installation in both the late-marque Spitfires and Seafires was essentially the same. (Eric B Morgan Collection)

Complete with a centreline drop tank is this Seafire F.17, SX345. Also clearly visible is the tail wheel wire guard and the shortness of the retracted arrestor hook. (Fleet Air Arm Museum)

of ground forces trying to flush out guerrilla forces from the Malayan jungle. Not only were the cannons used for attack purposes against specified targets, but to reinforce each attack the aircraft fired up to eight 60-pound unguided rockets at the same target point.

A transfer to sea duty in February 1950 saw No. 800 Sqdn and its Seafires embarking aboard HMS *Triumph* in company with the Fairey Fireflys of No. 827 Sqdn for a series of goodwill visits. It was during this tour that a fault in the design of the rear fuselage structure first appeared. Under normal circumstances, the Seafire on landing and taking the wire would run out for a near perfect landing. However, any misalignment resulted in excessive side loads being applied to the structure which in turn caused distortion and wrinkling of the aircraft's skin. Another problem occasionally experienced by pilots was that of undercarriage damage due to pilots misjudging the weight of the Seafire.

On 25 June 1950 the forces of North Korea invaded the territory claimed and defended by the south. This action resulted in condemnation by the United Nations and promises of support from the United States and its allies. Amongst the forces committed to driving out the North

Preparing the Seafires of No. 1832 Sqdn for flight. As a reserve unit normally based on land at Royal Naval Air Station Culham, this carrier shot is most unusual. Of note are the still drooped wingtips on the nearest example. These will be manually locked in place later. (Fleet Air Arm Museum)

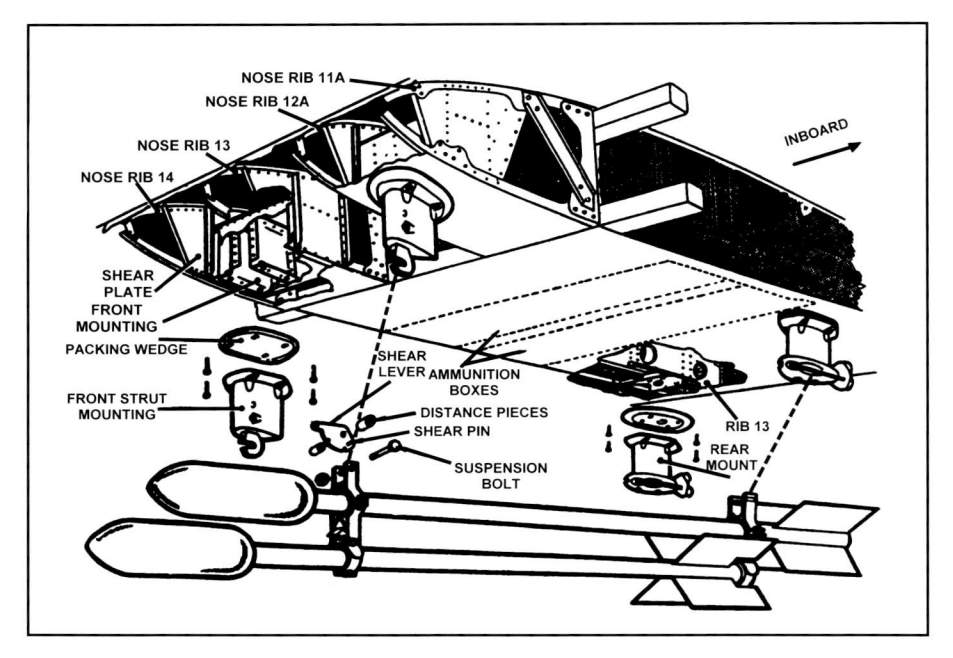

This diagram illustrates well the underwing rocket installation fitted to the Seafire FR.47. (Eric B Morgan Collection)

Korean insurgents were the aircraft embarked aboard HMS *Triumph*. By 2 July the carrier had joined U.S. Navy Task Force 77 headed by the USS *Valley Forge*. The first offensive operations launched by the air wing were against the enemy airfields near the North Korean capital, Pyongyang. As HMS *Triumph* was not equipped with quickly reloadable catapults, the strike aircraft of the FAA relied on RATOG to assist the first aircraft to depart the deck, the remainder leaving under their own power.

On this first mission nine Seafire FR.47s attacked the designated targets with little resistance from enemy forces. Two aircraft, however, suffered some minor damage, one

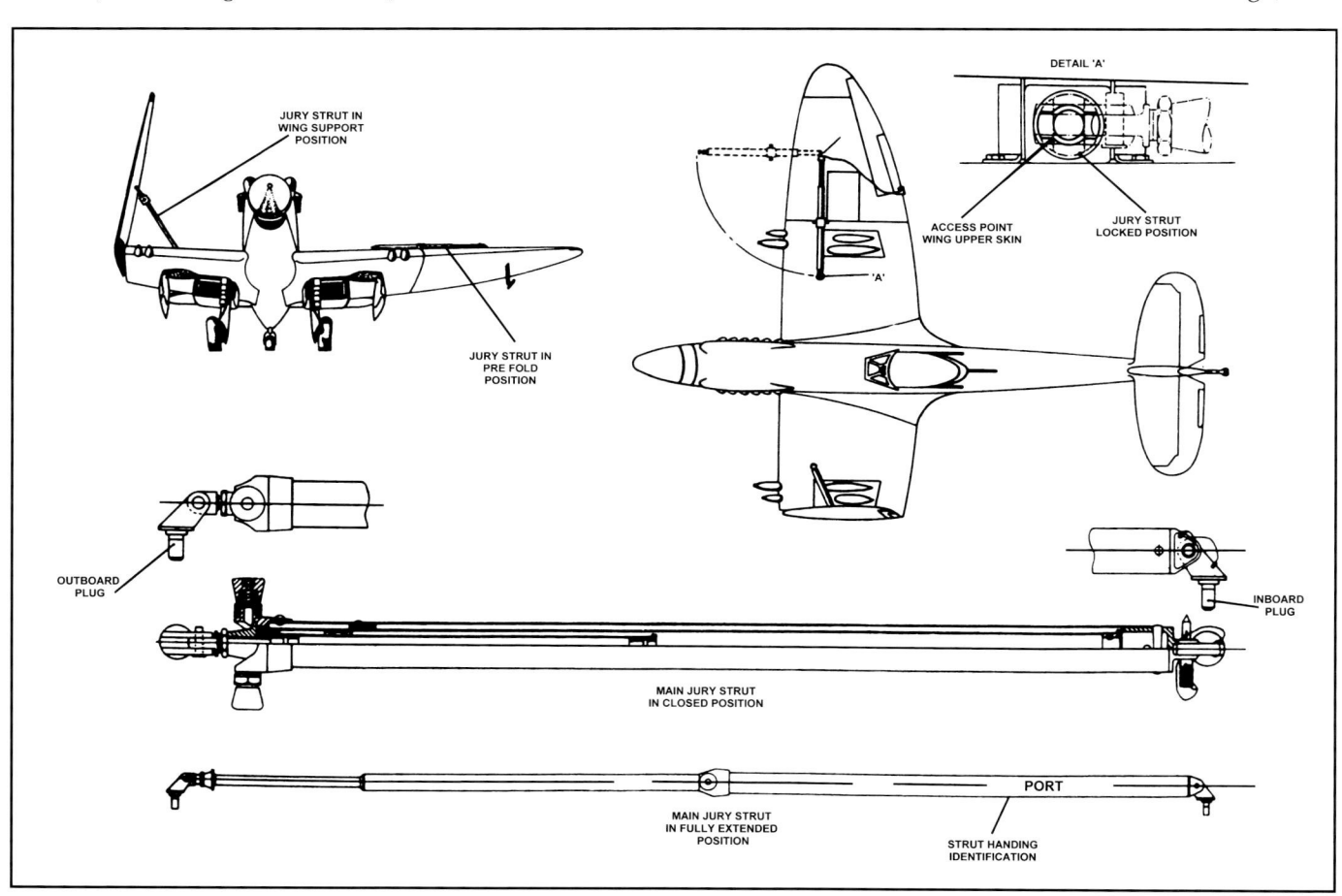

Aircraft operated by the Fleet Air Arm on aircraft carriers with folding wings required jury struts to support the structure when folded and protect them from overstress by wind power. (Big Bird Aviation Collection)

86

hit by rifle fire whilst the other was damaged by debris from its own rocket launches. On 4 July a force that included seven Seafires attacked targets on the railway network between Yonan and Haeju without loss. On completion of these missions Task Force 77 withdrew for a period of rectification and reappraisal of its role.

One change from the original plan was that the Seafire FR.47's would be responsible for Combat Air Patrol (CAP) in support of the U.S. Navy aircraft and for fleet defence. For these roles the aircraft would normally carry full cannon armament, a 50-gallon centreline tank, and a 22-gallon combat tank under each wing. This load inevitably reduced the top speed of the aircraft by some 25 mph although pilots were instructed not to jettison anything except in case of emergency. The rear fuselage defect was also cleared for active service as the aircraft were desperately needed for operations.

After a mainly uneventful tour of duty, HMS *Triumph* departed the war zone for a period of refurbishment in Japan. It later returned to blockade patrol off the North Korean coast on 11 August. From that point onward the Seafires of No. 800 Sqdn returned to multiple mission status by adding the full repertoire of ground attack missions to that of CAP. In addition to these flights, the squadron also provided escort aircraft and flew armed photo reconnaissance sorties.

The final Seafire FR.47 combat sortie was flown on 20 September after which HMS *Triumph* departed the area and returned to the UK. During its 11 weeks of combat flying the squadron had used 26 airframes, but by the end of operations only three were declared serviceable enough to continue flying. Of those declared unfit for further flying some were struck of charge, the greater majority of these being those aircraft that had suffered rear fuselage damage during landing.

The Seafires of No. 800 Sqdn had flown 360 sorties during their part in the Korean War without loss, although two were written off in noncombat accidents. No. 800 Sqdn finally dispensed with its Seafire FR.47s during November 1950 after which a handful were passed to No. 759 Sqdn for fighter conversion duties, in which role they served until November 1953. One other unit was to operate the FR.47 before it finally left the service of the FAA. This was No. 1833 Sqdn, RNVR which re-equipped in June 1952 at its base of Bramcote near Nottingham. This final unit to fly the type retained its ten aircraft until it finally retired from the FAA in 1954.

After Korea No. 800 Sqdn relinquished its Seafires to such units as No. 1832 Sqdn of the Royal Naval Volunteer Reserve. This is a Seafire FR.47 of that unit awaiting its next pilot. The slight offset of the camera reveals both the upper fuselage oblique camera ports. (Fleet Air Arm Museum)

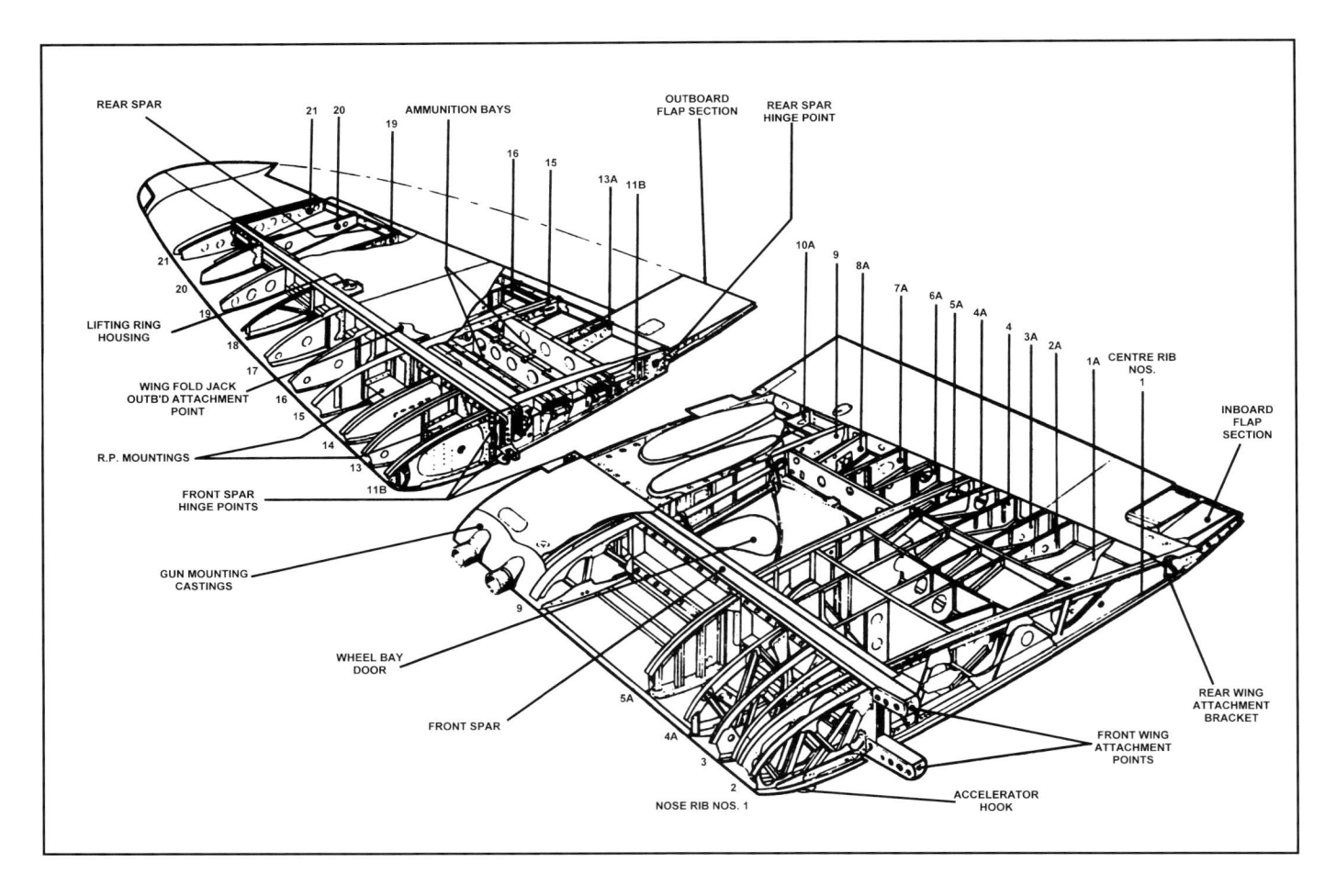

This diagram illustrates quite clearly the power fold mechanism fitted to the greater majority of Seafire FR.47s. Earlier-built aircraft were entirely manual in operation. (Eric B Morgan Collection)

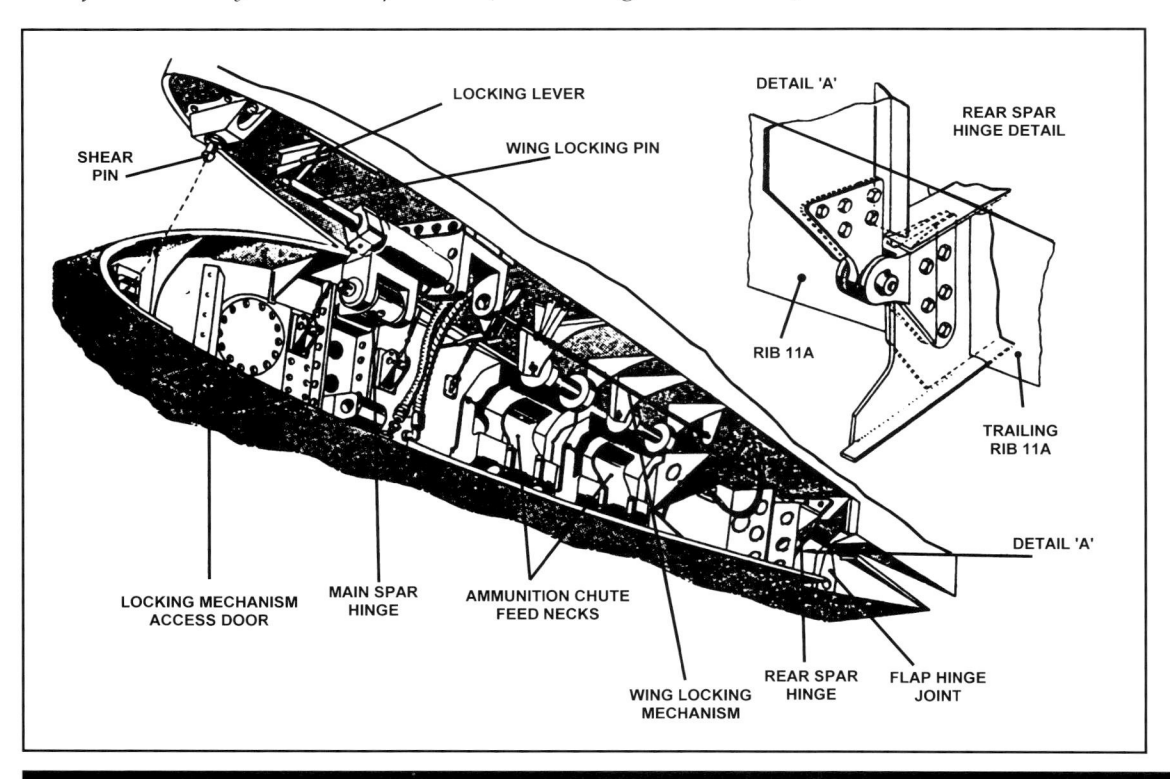

The Seafire FR.47 wing fold mechanism is well illustrated in this close-up diagram. This is the powered version. (Eric B Morgan Collection)

After their service, many of the redundant Seafire FR.47s were placed in storage to await final disposal. VP485 is sitting parked with its wings folded and shows quite clearly the enlarged tail unit and contra-rotating propeller fitted to this version. (C P Russell Smith Collection)

Complete with underwing rockets and Rocket Assisted Take Off Gear this Seafire FR.47 of No. 800 Sqdn Fleet Air Arm begins its takeoff run. Of note is the open canopy regarded as essential should the aircraft encounter problems. (Fleet Air Arm Museum)

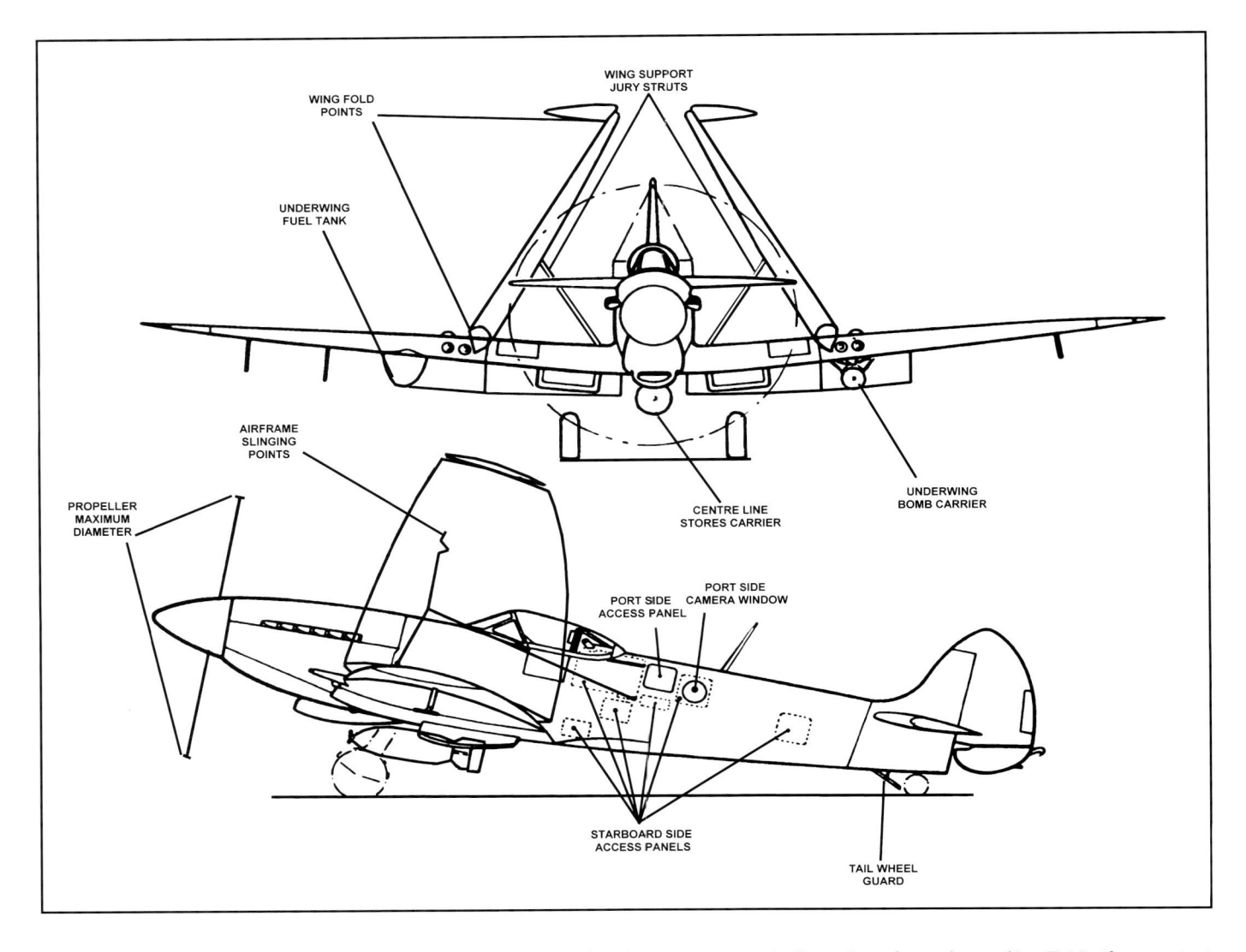

This general arrangement of the Seafire FR.47 reveals that it was a very similar aircraft to the earlier F.46, the greatest difference being the incorporation of wing folding in the former. (Big Bird Aviation Collection)

Equipped with Rocket Assisted Take Off Gear this Seafire FR.47 of No. 800 Sqdn Fleet Air Arm, complete with Korea war zone striping, departs the carrier for another Combat Air Patrol. (Fleet Air Arm Museum)

This undersurface photo of a Seafire FR.47 approaching to land reveals a wealth of detail. Noteworthy are the modified undercarriage units of the second generation of Griffon Seafires, the intake fairing which stops just short of the spinner, and the location of the underwing fuel tanks. (Fleet Air Arm Museum)

Contact — and this Seafire F.17 successfully engages the wire on touchdown aboard HMS Pretoria Castle. *Of note are the fully deployed flaps which were only used for landing purposes. (Fleet Air Arm Museum)*

This close-up shot of a Griffon Seafire reveals a wealth of detail, not only of its occupants, but the aircraft itself. Clearly defined are the engine bearer beams, the rearview mirror, the reinforced wing root walkway, and the cockpit access door. (Fleet Air Arm Museum)

Seafire F.46, LA550, was one of the few that saw some use by the Fleet Air Arm, this being at Royal Naval Air Station Ford. Prominent in this view are the outboard undercarriage doors inherited from the equivalent Griffon Spitfires. (C P Russell Smith Collection)

FINAL FLING

THE SPITEFUL AND THE SEAFANG

By the time the Spiteful and Seafang came to light from Supermarine the day of the piston-engined fighter had almost passed, their replacement by jet aircraft being a certainty. However, the development of the jet engine, in both centrifugal or axial forms, was subject to improving their reliability. Before that happened, Vickers Supermarine was determined to take the Spitfire design to one last stage.

In contrast to earlier versions of the Spitfire, the new variant was subjected to extensive development, especially in the field of aerodynamic behaviour. Also to feature in this new aircraft were laminar flow wings which, in theory, would give a marked increase in speed over the original design for the Spitfire range. There is of course a problem with such aerofoils in that they are very susceptible to marks caused by military boots, dead insects, paintwork damage, and panel distortion, all of which had a tendency to eliminate any of the benefits gained. For example, a grain that measured 0.0022 inches could reduce the top speed by as much as 43 mph on an airframe rated at 380 mph.

The foregoing notwithstanding, Supermarine, in conjunction with Rolls Royce and encouraged by the RAF and the MoS, began the complex process of designing such an aircraft which could operate quite happily at speeds in excess of 400 mph. First attempts at investigating this last vestige of the Spitfire were undertaken by the RAE in 1942 using a pair of Merlin-powered Spitfire Mk.IXs. These development flights frequently reached Mach 0.86 which exceeded the airframe's set "never to exceed speed" of Mach 0.85.

The performance of these airframes gave the development team a set of initial parameters to work from, the first of which was that the wing

Making its first flight on 2 April 1945, the first production Spiteful F.XIV is seen here posing at height for the camera. By this time the enlarged tail unit had been fitted to counteract the torque generated by the Griffon engine. (Eric B Morgan Collection)

would need extensive redesigning to eliminate the drag curves created by following the National Advisory Committee on Aeronautics (NACA) 2200 aerofoil. Although this shape was adequate for the Merlin-powered aircraft and the first vestiges of the Griffon range, they were overcambered for the lift coefficients needed for the new aircraft and the speed range it was required to operate in.

Further development flying was undertaken using a Spitfire F.21 which was Griffon engined and had a refined wing planform to set a more advanced range of parameters at sea level. Even this aircraft and its follow-on versions would eventually become limited by the compressibility of the wing which, from Supermarine's point of view, would be very embarrassing.

These resulted in the Air Staff issuing requirements for two types of aircraft to Supermarine to further develop the concept. The first of these to fly was the Type 372 which materialised in the form of Spitfire Mk.VIII, JG204. This airframe featured a normal Spitfire wing with its leading edge lifted slightly in an effort to increase speed. Redesignated the F.23 the overall speed increase of 4 mph was not deemed enough to justify series production. The second line of research was encapsulated in the Type 371 which was seen from the outset as a totally new design destined for quantity production.

With that end in mind the wing was designed with a taper to both leading and trailing edges. Further calculations by the Aerodynamics Department at Supermarine revealed that a wing with a span of 35 feet, giving a surface area of 210 square feet, would suffice to do the job.

With assistance from the National Physics Laboratory (NPL), which joined the project at the end of 1942, the thickness chord ratio was set at 13 percent at the wing root which would give accommodation for the main undercarriage. Such modifica-

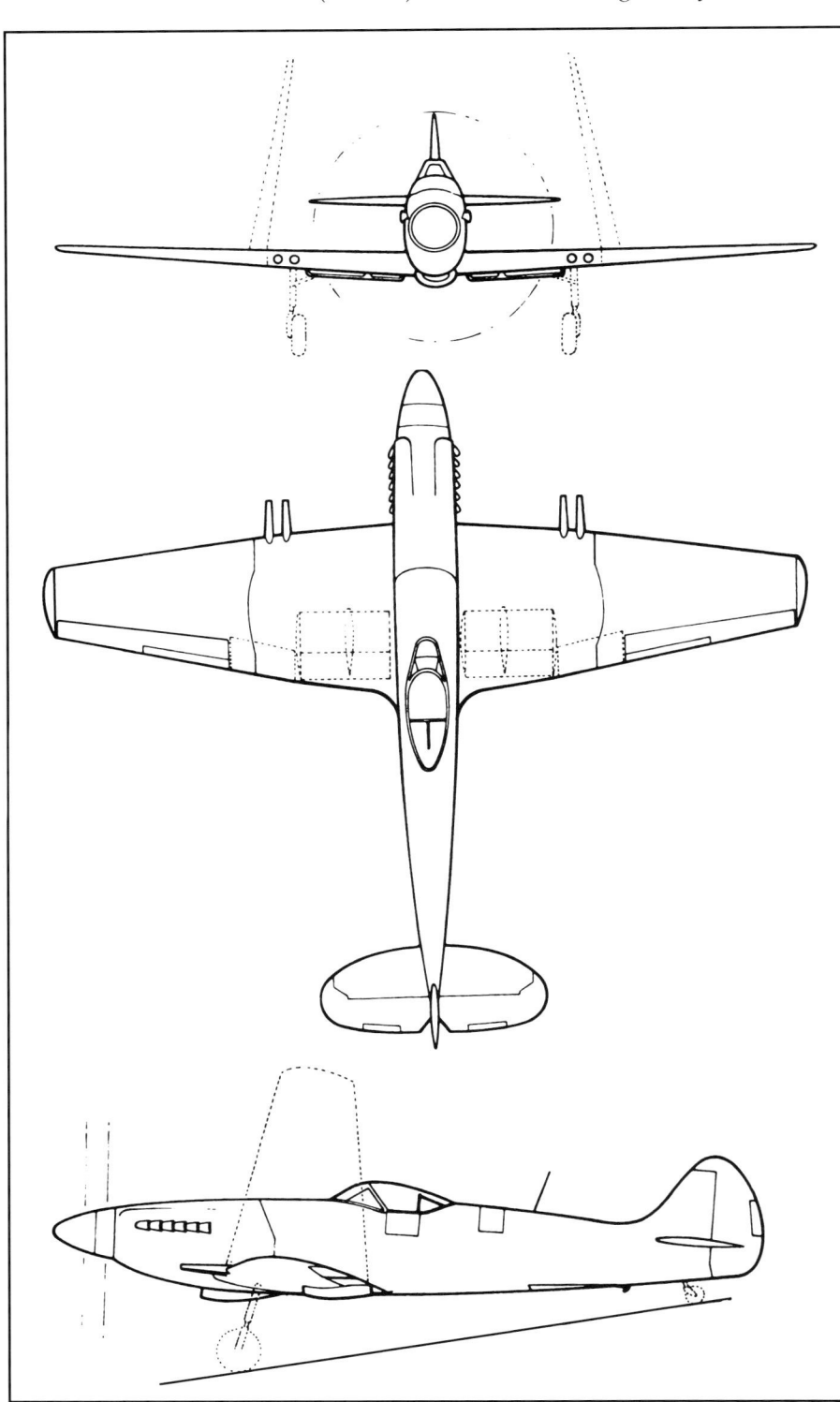

This diagram illustrates the first Seafang that was converted from a Spiteful. Of note is the wide track undercarriage. (Eric B Morgan Collection)

tions to the design actually removed the inner wing section from being a pure laminar flow wing although the outer part of the wing did comply.

When the design was settled, Supermarine issued its own specification, No. 470, in late 1942 to define the new wing characteristics prior to production. This projected that the design would achieve the highest critical speed possible before compressibility became a problem, that it would have the highest rate of roll of any fighter ever built, and that the wing profile drag should be reduced as much as possible to increase performance. All these parameters, when measured against an existing set of F.21 data, would reveal that the critical mach number had been raised from Mach 0.64 to Mach 0.72 which was a real speed increase of 55 mph.

When the blueprints were prepared they revealed a component that was easier than previous designs to manufacture. It featured tapers to both edges of the wing plus thicker skinning. Thicker skin served two purposes. One was to increase the wing's strength and thus reduce the chance of distortion. The other purpose involved an issue of stiffness, in that high torsional rigidity would be provided thus allowing good aileron control at very high speeds. This in turn would guarantee that aileron reversal would not occur until at least 850 mph. Estimated speeds in comparison with the F.21 were 470 mph at 39,500 feet for the fighter whilst the Type 371 wing would achieve 504 mph at the same height.

With the research complete, the Air Ministry felt justified in issuing Specification F.1/43 for a single-seat, single-engined fighter incorporating the laminar wing. Subparagraphs within this specification called for the wing to be available for fitting to the F.21 without modification and that it should be available for installation on a version of the aircraft for the FAA.

The primary difference between both versions would be the installation of wing folding mechanisms. The fuselage was based on the Mk.VIII, later

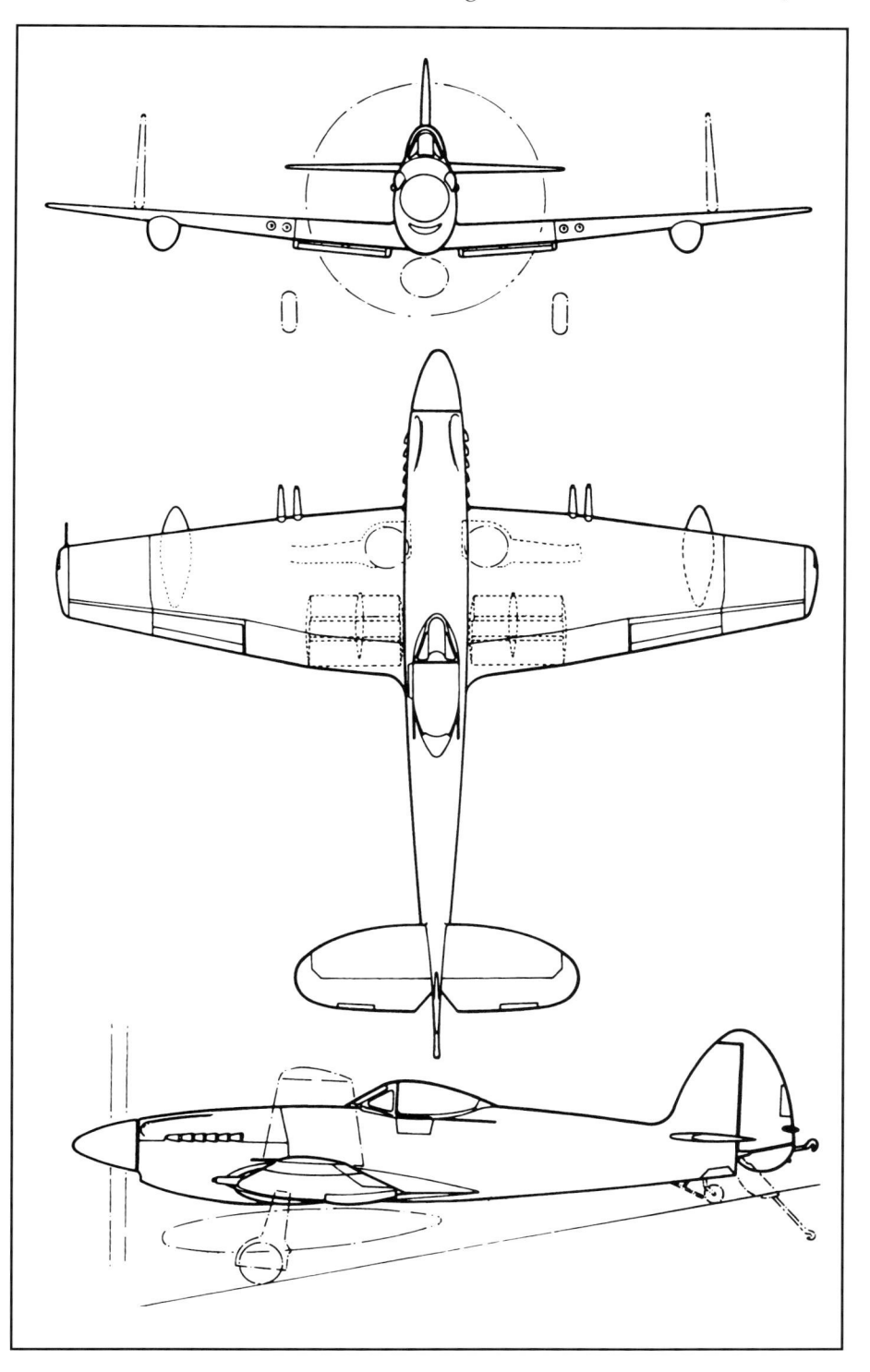

The fully navalised Seafang featured a sting tailhook, fitments for a centreline fuel tank, and the blended external wing tanks first seen on the Seafire FR.47. (Eric B Morgan Collection)

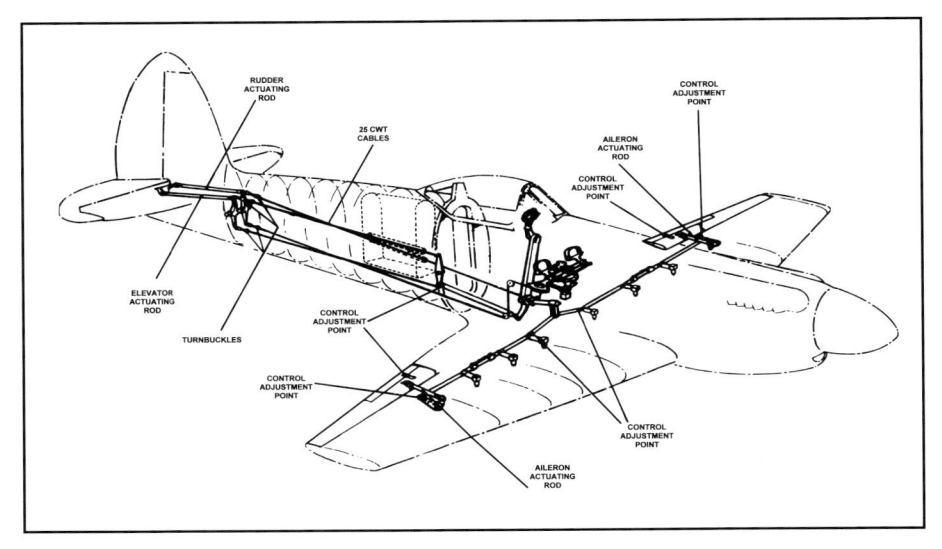

The flight control system fitted into the Spiteful and Seafang was based on that fitted to the later mark Spitfires and Seafires. (Eric B Morgan Collection)

changed to that of the F.XIV, into which would be fitted an R-R Griffon powerplant which would in turn drive a pair of three-bladed propeller assemblies driving in a contra-rotating direction.

As the development of materials had improved during the previous years of conflict, the specification of a bubble hood canopy was stated as a requirement from the outset. In the original specification there was a clause that stated that a Merlin could be fitted instead although this option was not exercised. Fuel contents within the new airframe were set at 149 gallons with 60 gallons possible in external overload tanks. Armament was specified as four 20mm Mark.V Hispano cannons. Also settled at this time was the aircraft's name which had passed through Valiant and Victor to end as Spiteful.

In contrast to the earlier versions of the Spitfire there was an intensive participation by the RAE and the NPL, both of which carried out intensive wind tunnel tests at every stage of the design. Other changes were an improvement in manufacturing tolerances as the new wing in particular would be very responsive to any production flaws. Precision manufacturing techniques were also required in the vicinity of removable panels where any airflow disturbance could reduce the aircraft's top speed considerably.

Test flights of the new wing were undertaken using Spitfire XIV, NN660, which made its maiden flight on 30 June 1944. Regarded as a hybrid prototype, this aircraft was powered by a Griffon 61 engine driving the standard five-blade propeller.

The operational life of this airframe was short as it crashed in September of that year during a mock air combat flight against a Spitfire XIV. Although a definite cause was never completely established it was suspected that the aileron control circuit had either been jammed or disconnected under positive G forces thus allowing flexure or jamming in the control runs to occur. Some indications of forthcoming problems experienced in early test flights where the wing at, or near, the stall had exhibited some unpleasant characteristics especially with aileron snatch.

Although the loss of NN660 was a tragedy, the production of the Spiteful was to continue. Thus it was on 8 January 1945 that the first prototype

This general arrangement of the Spiteful reveals the layout of the laminar wing planform. (Eric B Morgan Collection)

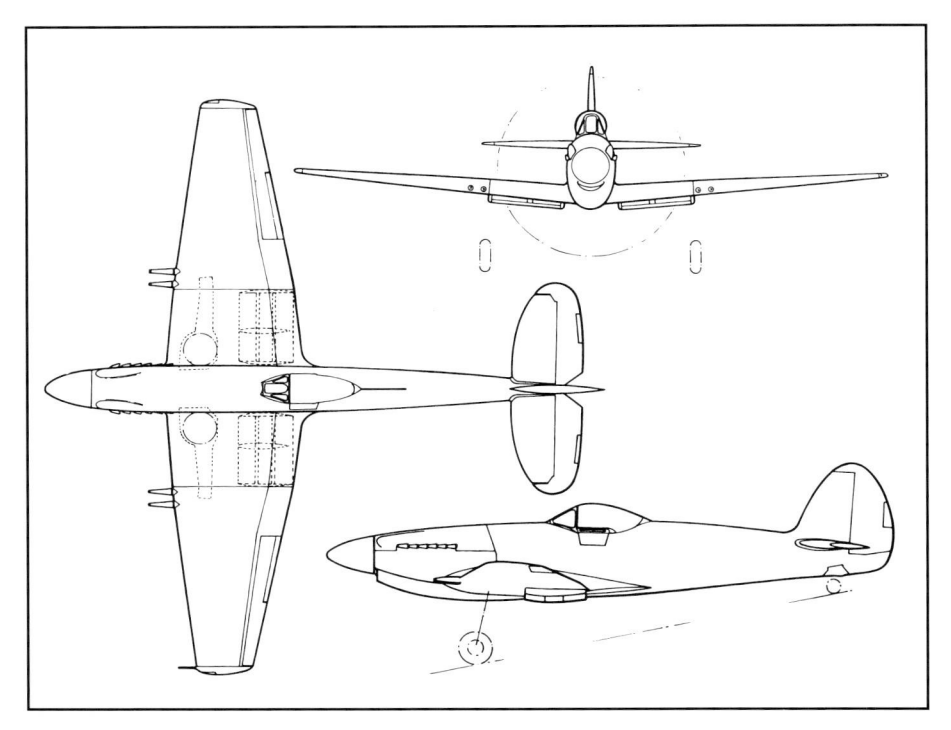

Spiteful, NN664, made its first flight complete with a redesigned aileron control circuit. The first requirements addressed in the early test flights were those of the ailerons snatching at speeds close to the stall, also noted was the tendency of the wing to drop at this point.

A further problem that occurred was the ineffectiveness of the ailerons under high G forces near the stall which resulted in a definite involuntary flick of the wings. Many of these faults were attributed to the design of the surfaces themselves. Efforts were concentrated on eradicating the faults.

Many ideas were tried, these included shortening the ailerons, modifying the wing surface near the surface, fitting beading to the trailing edge which changed the airflow, slotted ailerons, and finally, wing spoilers. None of these effectively cured the problem, therefore further investigation was required. This subsequently revealed that the fitment of an enlarged tail unit would restore the authority of the ailerons. The new configuration was first flown on 24 June 1945.

Also at this time serious consideration was given to fitting an ejection seat to assist the pilot in escaping should the need arise. Much of the cockpit development work had been undertaken using a wooden mock up which had enabled the design team to try various control layouts and other ideas before metal was cut.

One of the less convincing ideas that found its way into the first Spiteful was an attempt to build a cockpit that would reduce the tendency of pilots to black out under high G forces. Although medically quite convincing, the whole idea was deemed impractical as the resulting setup, complete with raised rudder pedals, was very uncomfortable and pilots of the FAA would have had great difficulty in seeing to land.

Whilst the problems afflicting the prototype were being cured, production had commenced of aircraft for frontline use. The first production airframe, RB515, made its maiden flight on 2 April 1945 fitted with the original F.21 style of tail unit. This was subsequently replaced by a Spiteful tail unit which was first air tested on 21 May. For reasons best known to the authorities, it was decided to start the number series at F.XIV when fitted with a Griffon 69 engine driving a five-bladed propeller.

Originally contract totals for 650 and 190 Spitefuls were ordered. This was swiftly reduced to just 17 at the cessation of hostilities. The final aircraft of this small production run was delivered on 17 January 1947. However, production of the necessary engines had reached 160, most of which were placed in storage. A handful were later diverted to the naval Seafang.

The FAA also had some influence on the engine intake for the carburettor slung beneath the powerplant. Originally this had been of the short variety and incorporated a tropical filter, but on the second prototype, NN667, this had been changed to the extended version first seen on the Seafire F.47. Built to a similar specification as the first prototype this aircraft suffered from all the handling faults that afflicted NN664.

When the production version of the Spiteful was authorised it was intended that the powerplant would be either a Griffon 89 or 90 engine driving a contra-rotating propeller and that this model would be designated the F.15. In the event this version was not built as delays in progressing the airframe, engine and propeller assemblies meant that the requirement for this aircraft had disappeared.

Only one other version of the new fighter was to be constructed, this

This photo of a Seafang F.32, VB895, clearly shows the radiator assemblies moved to the trailing edge of the wing plus the undercarriage units that were to feature on the later Supermarine Attacker. (Fleet Air Arm Museum)

The last vestige of the Spitfire genre came to fruition with the Supermarine Attacker which borrowed the wings and undercarriage from the redundant Spiteful series of aircraft. Contrast this photo with that of the Supermarine S.6 at the beginning of this book to really understand the evolution of this most famous of fighters. (C P Russell Smith Collection)

was the F.16 of which only one was produced. This was serialled RB518 and flew with a Griffon 101 engine fitted with a two-stage three-speed supercharger which in turn drove a five-bladed propeller.

Although designated as a pure fighter, the Seafang F.32 was clearly equipped for the photo reconnaissance role as the oblique camera ports reveal. Although destined never to see any frontline service, both the Spiteful and Seafang were smooth, clean aircraft which handled well overall. (Fleet Air Arm Museum)

Very much a conglomeration, this airframe retained the original short intake, but was fitted with a Seafang bubble hood and windscreen. Used mainly as a trials machine, RB518 was found to be at least 10 mph slower than the standard F.XIV version, although it was no slouch as it managed 447 mph at 25,500 feet increasing to 494 mph at 27,800 feet which made it the fastest British piston-powered aircraft ever built. RB518 was the subject of further trials involving both engines and propellers.

One of the first combinations evaluated was a five-bladed NACA profile propeller which allowed the Spiteful to reach a maximum speed of 487 mph. Another evaluation undertaken using RB518 was of a Clark Y section contra-rotating propeller. This was driven by a Griffon 121 engine which was specifically configured for contra-rotating propellers. Under test flight conditions the aircraft achieved 470 mph in level flight at 30,000 feet.

Investigation of the reduction in top speed was attributed to the powerplant, although it was not possible to evaluate the problem as RB518 was to suffer a major engine failure whilst undertaking a test flight. The ensuing crash landing at Chilbolton effectively wrote off this airframe, especially as it was dropped later by the recovery crane, reducing it to scrap. Having suffered a series of engine failures whilst testing the Griffon 101/121 engines, the loss of RB518 effectively killed the Spiteful programme.

Of the remaining 16 production airframes built, 13 were sold for scrap in 1948 having only flown sufficient hours to clear the aircraft by the manufacturer and to deliver it to No. 6 Maintenance Unit (MU) at RAF

Brize Norton for storage. Of the remaining airframes, RB520 was allocated to the Seafang development programme for which purpose it was fitted with a sting-type arrestor hook.

There was even an attempt to sell the type overseas, Switzerland having expressed a strong interest. So much so in fact that a group of pilots were sent to the UK to evaluate the Spiteful which they reported upon favourably. However, the ability of British bureaucracy to interfere with aircraft exports managed to wreck the firm's chances of a sale.

Technical specifications of the Spiteful were as follows: The span was 35 feet 6 inches with a wing area of 210 square feet. The fuselage length of the F.14 and F.16 was 32 feet 4 inches whilst that of the F.15 was seven inches longer. The powerplant for all versions was the Griffon 90 for the five-bladed aircraft whilst that of the contra-rotating variety was from the 101/121 series. All were started using the Coffman cartridge starter. Fuel capacity totalled 178 gallons internally with the capacity to carry an extra 90 or 180 gallons in external overload tanks. Range using normal internal fuel was 564 miles whilst the greatest speed in a dive reached 525 mph. In contrast, the stall speed was 95 mph. The armament for the Spiteful included four Mark.V Hispano 20mm cannons with a total of 674 rounds whilst externally the carriage of two 1,000-pound bombs or alternately four 300-pound rocket projectiles could be carried.

The navalised version of the Spiteful, the Seafang, was very much a nonstarter although, had the hostilities in Europe continued, orders for this aircraft would have undoubtedly been large. Designated the Type 382 by Supermarine, the Seafang was to feature folding wings, a sting-type arrestor hook, structural strengthening for the undercarriage

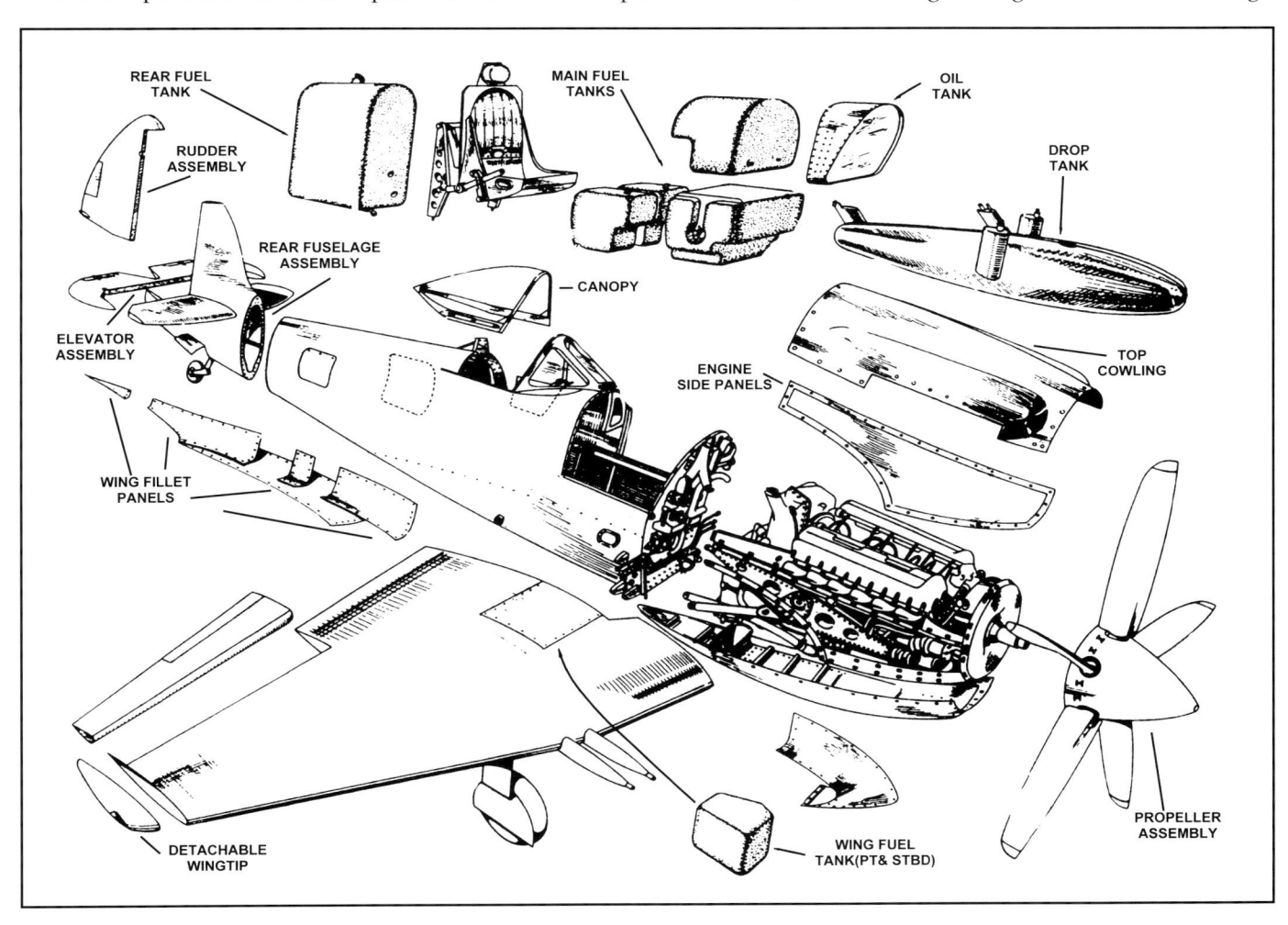

The Spiteful and Seafang shared many major components that are illustrated in this assembly drawing. (Eric B Morgan Collection)

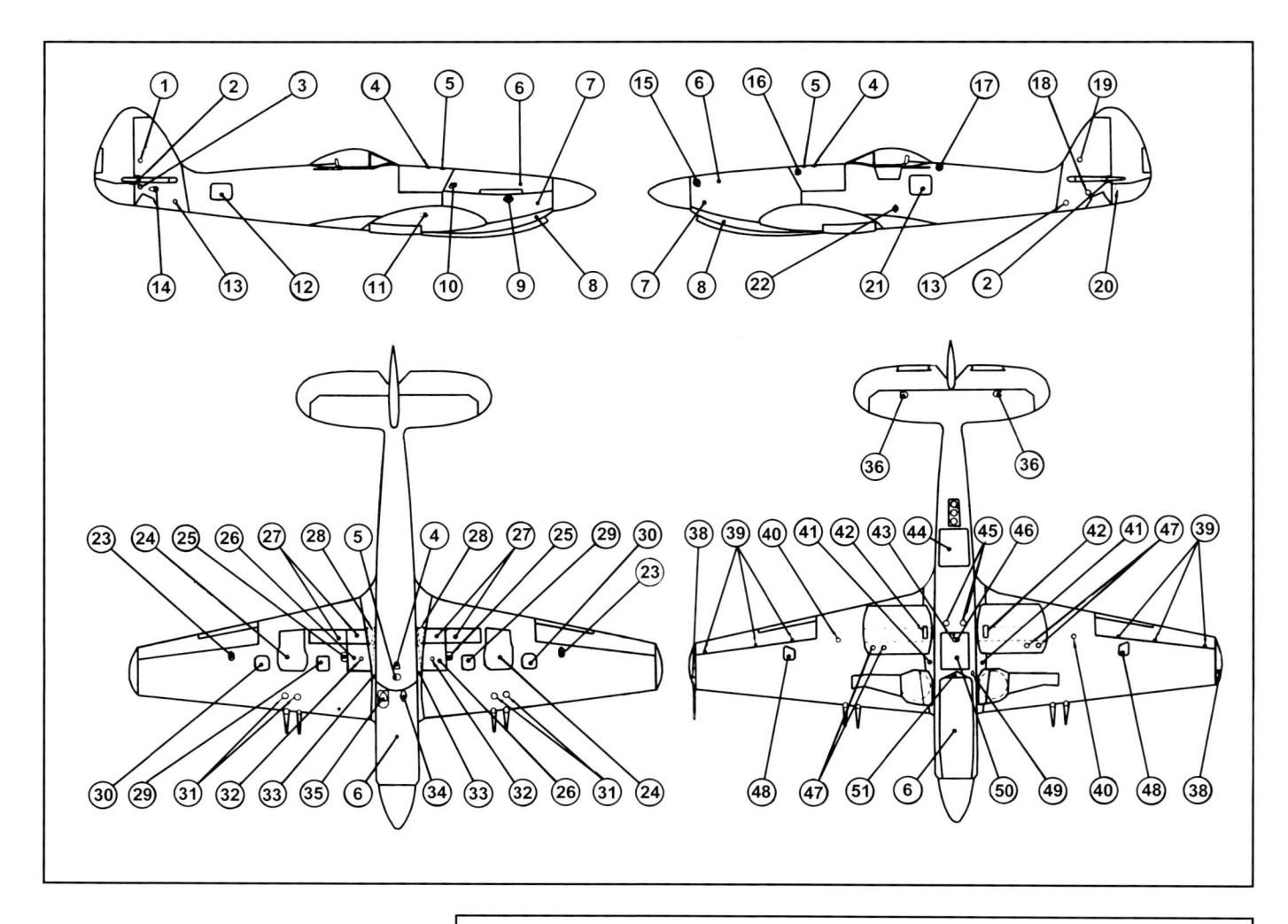

Although a small aircraft, the Spiteful was well catered for with access panels. (Eric B Morgan Collection)

1 RUDDER TAB SCREW JACK	27 RADIATOR MOUNTING
2 ELEVATOR GAP	28 ELECTRICAL CONNECTIONS
3 ELEVATOR TRIM TAB CONNECTION	29 INBOARD AMMUNITION BOX
4 FUEL FILLER CAP	30 OUTBOARD AMMUNITION BOX
5 OIL FILLER CAP	31 GUN GAS PLUGS
6 TOP COWLING PANEL	32 FUEL TANK FILLER CAP
7 SIDE COWLING PANEL	33 WING ROOT CONNECTIONS
8 BOTTM COWLING PANEL	34 HYDRAULIC RESERVOIR & CHARGING VALVE
9 ENGINE STARTER BREECH	35 INTERCOOLER HEADER TANK
10 GEARBOX DIPSTICK	36 ELEVATOR TRIM TAB SCREW JACKS
11 FIELD TANK CONNECTIONS	37 IDENTIFICATION LAMPS
12 DR COMPASS/REAR FUSELAGE	38 WINGTIP LAMP TERMINAL BLOCK
13 FLYING CONTROLS/TAILWHEEL UNIT	39 AILERON HINGES
14 ELEVATOR TRIM TAB	40 AILERON CONTROL & FLAP JACK
15 MAIN COOLANT HEADER TANK	41 WING ROOT CONNECTIONS
16 OIL FILLER CAP	42 RADIATOR DRAIN PLUGS
17 REAR TANK FILLER CAP	43 COCKPIT DRAIN
18 TAILWHEEL STRUT	44 REAR FUEL TANK
19 RUDDER TRIM TAB CONTROLS	45 SADDLE TANK DRAIN PLUGS
20 LOWER RUDDER HINGE	46 HYDRAULIC SYSTEM DRAIN PLUGS
21 RADIO	47 PIPE CONNECTIONS
22 ELECT GROUND SUPPLY SOCKET	48 AILERON CONTROLS
23 AILERON ACTUATING ROD	49 SUPERCHARGER DRAIN
24 GUN AND AILERON CONTROL	50 MAIN FUEL TANK
25 RADIATOR FLAP JACK	51 BOTTOM COWLING
26 AILERON CONTROLS	

units, plus all the other revisions needed to create a navalised fighter. To cater to the new aircraft, Specification No. 5/45 was issued on 21 April 1945 by the Air Ministry. However, the FAA was very reluctant to accept the new Supermarine offering as it was seen as inferior to the DH Sea Hornet and Hawker Sea Fury which were already in service. These objections notwithstanding, two development airframes, VB893 and 895, were ordered.

Supermarine had already produced a prototype for the Seafang programme by fitting a Spiteful, RB520, with an arrestor hook. Vickers Supermarine then undertook trials at the test airfield at High Post before declaring the aircraft ready for service collection. Two years later, after being left unused in storage, the aircraft was collected on behalf of the FAA and then struck of service charge.

Although the converted Spiteful was never used in the test sequence, the two development airframes were. Thus at the beginning of 1946, VB895 undertook its maiden flight designated as the Seafang Mk.XXXII. Fitted with power folding wings and a Griffon 89 that drove a five-bladed propeller, the Seafang underwent manufacturer's trials before departing to Farnborough for trials and service evaluation.

During this period most of the test flights concerned simulated deck landings and revealed a weakness in the rudder balance horn. After various unsuccessful attempts to strengthen this assembly the entire rudder and its mountings were completely redesigned.

Further deck landing trials were carried out at Chilbolton and the shore establishment RNAS Ford where the behaviour of the Seafang during landing was praised. Its wide-track landing gear made the aircraft exceptionally stable on the ground. Some actual carrier landing trials were later carried out on HMS *Illustrious* after which the aircraft returned to shore-based use.

After the successful conclusion of the landing trials, attention was turned to the performance of the external fuel tanks, especially during drop trials. These were modified from earlier models and allowed the front end of the tank to drop upon pulling of the release mechanism. As it pulled clear, the electrical and fuel feeds disconnected and the airflow would then pull the tank clear of the rear mounts. Both 90-gallon and 170-gallon tanks were tested up to an airspeed of 255 mph.

Prior to the delivery of the aircraft allocated to these trials, another airframe had been delivered to Farnborough. This, the sixth airframe, VG741, was designated Mk.31 and was delivered to Farnborough on 15 January 1946 for trials. In contrast to the other Seafangs, this particular machine lacked folding wings and was fitted with a five-bladed propeller.

Another aircraft from this batch, VG474, was used to trial Lockheed servodynes in November 1947 requiring the removal of the rear fuselage fuel tanks. Overall the system was praised although the pilots did mention that the control column had a tendency to creep to full travel instead of a sudden sharp movement. Further trials were undertaken to determine the type's available mach number which reached a maximum of 0.77 although the Seafang was noted as unstable at speeds approaching Mach 0.75.

A later series of trials concerning VB895 covered the operation of a new gun bay ventilation system which drew its cooling air through leading edge intakes and vented it out via dump pipes located on the gun bay panels. This modification had been required to combat the build up of unstable gases in the bay which had resulted in explosions in the wing.

Although a total of 150 aircraft were ordered, only nine complete Seafangs were delivered whilst a further seven were delivered in knockdown kit form. This order had originally been for an equivalent number of Spitefuls although the end of hostilities had changed the initial requirement. Of this total, a few were used for development and trials uses as mentioned before whilst the remainder were sold off for scrap. The laminar flow wing, however, lived on in another Supermarine product. The Attacker jet-powered attack fighter eventually entered FAA service in reasonable quantities.

This was originally known as the Jet Spiteful for which the naval requirement E.10/44 was issued under a MAP specification in mid-1944. The concept behind the aircraft was to use the wings from the Spiteful, for which Supermarine was already tooled to produce, and ally them to a basically circular fuselage. This structure contained the pilot in a slender forward fuselage whilst the designated powerplant was developed from a Rolls Royce centrifugal jet engine later named the "Nene."

Test flights of the prototype, TS409, began in July 1946 and revealed an aircraft that handled very well except for a touch of elevator heaviness. This was later cured by the use of a spring tab. As only one prototype had been constructed, the design team recommended that a tricycle undercarriage be fitted on production aircraft. After consultation with the Admiralty, this concept was abandoned as the Navy required a tail wheel jet aircraft to prove the concept before introducing nose wheel airframes to aircraft carriers. Eventually, Supermarine built some nosewheel aircraft for both the RAF and the FAA in the shape of the Swift and the Scimitar.

During this period there were some overseas enquiries concerning sales of the Seafang from the Royal Netherlands Navy plus others from the French and American armed forces. Although some evaluation flying was undertaken, no sales were forthcoming, thus both the Spiteful and the Seafang were unable to fulfil their obvious sales potential.

Spitfire Alphabet

Acronyms and Abbreviations

2 TAF	2nd Tactical Air Force	FEAF	Far East Air Force	RAF	Royal Air Force
A&AEE	Aircraft and Armament Experimental Establishment	GP	General Purpose	R Aux AF	Royal Auxiliary Air Force
		HMS	His/ Her Majesty's Ship	RATOG	Rocket Assisted Take Off Gear
AFDU	Air Fighting Development Unit	MoS	Ministry of Supply	RCAF	Royal Canadian Air Force
AFS	Advanced Flying School	MU	Maintenance Unit	REAF	Royal Egyptian Air Force
AUW	All Up Weight	NACA	National Advisory Committee on Aeronautics	RNAS	Royal Naval Air Station
BAFO	British Armed Forces Overseas	NPL	National Physics Laboratory	RNVR	Royal Naval Volunteer Reserve
BEF	British Expeditionary Force			R-R	Rolls Royce
		OCU	Operational Conversion Unit	R Swe AF	Royal Swedish Air Force
CAM	Catapult Armed Merchantman	OTU	Operational Training Unit	SEAC	South East Asian Command
CAP	Combat Air Patrol			THUM	Temperature and Humidity Flight
CFE	Central Flying Establishment	PRU	Photo Reconnaissance Unit	TT	Target Tug
DH	De Havilland	PRDU	Photo Reconnaissance Development Unit	UHF	Ultra High Frequency
DTD	Directorate of Technical Development			USS	United States Ship
		RAE	Royal Aeronautical Establishment	USAAF	United States Army Air Forces
FAA	Fleet Air Arm				

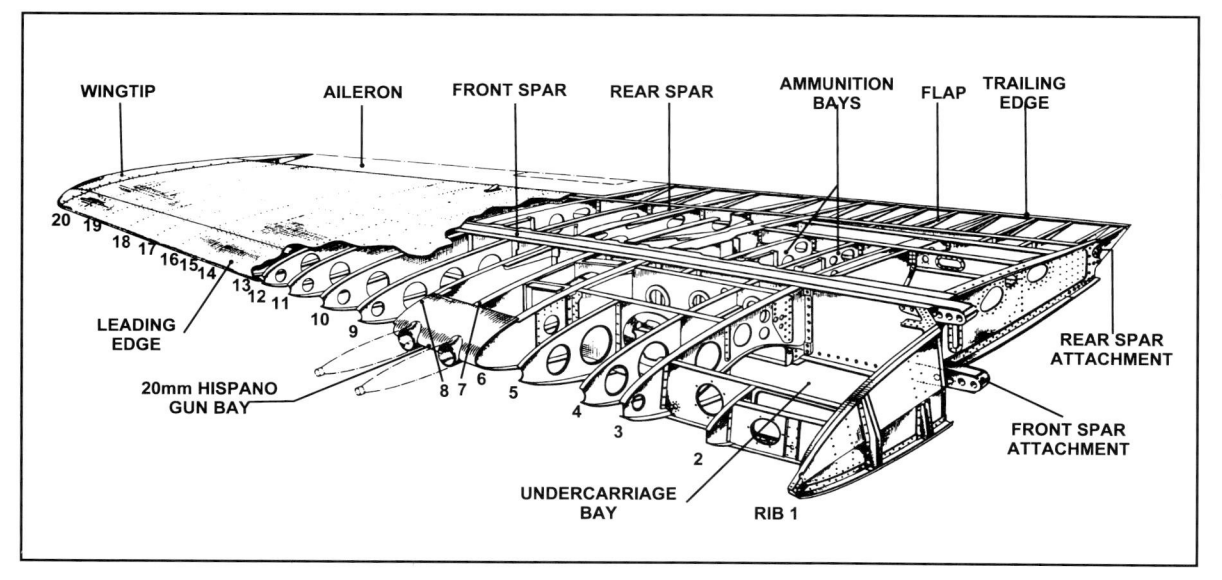

Internally, the laminar wing fitted to both the Spiteful and Seafang was much simpler in comparison with the earlier Spitfire and Seafire. (Eric B Morgan Collection)

Significant Dates

Key Dates in the History of the Griffon-Powered Spitfire

18 September 1931
Supermarine S6B seaplane achieves World Airspeed Record of 379 mph.

February 1934
First flight of Supermarine Type 224, the link between the S6B and the Spitfire.

5 March 1935
First flight of prototype F.37/34, K5054, later to be named the Spitfire.

14 May 1938
First flight of production Spitfire Mk.1.

13 October 1942
Maiden flight of Type 366 Spitfire Mk.XII to contract B19713/39 dated 23 August 1941. This contract was originally for Spitfire Mk.Vc aircraft.

February 1943
No. 41 Sqdn RAF equipped with Spitfire Mk.XII.

24 April 1943
First deliveries of second batch of Spitfire Mk.XII to the same contract number dated 12 May 1942. This batch of aircraft was based on the Spitfire Mk.VIII, whilst the first contract was based on the Mk.Vc. A total of 100 aircraft were built.

October 1943
Maiden flight of Supermarine Type 369/373/379 prototype which preceded the production examples of the F.XIV, F.XVIII, and reconnaissance variants ordered under contract B980385/39 dated 27 July 1942. The contract originally covered an order for Spitfire Mk.VIII aircraft.

January 1944
No. 610 Sqdn equips with Spitfire F.XIV. A total of 957 versions of the F.XIV were built.

27 January 1944
Type 368, designated Spitfire F.21, undertakes its maiden flight. The original contract, B981687/39, dated March 1942, was for Spitfire Mk.Vc aircraft. A final number of 120 airframes were built.

25 February 1944
First flight of Supermarine Type 377/386 as Seafire XV. Contract A/C 2777/c.23(c) was originally issued to cover order for Seafire III dated July 1943. It was followed by definitive contract B124305/40 dated February 1944. A final total of 390 aircraft were built.

June 1944
Supermarine Type 398 Seafire XVII contracts issued for conversion of one prototype F.XV to the new standard. Contract numbers AIR/2777/C.23(c) and AIR/3853. These aircraft, 232 in total, were built by Westland and Cunliffe Owen.

17 January 1945
Maiden flight of Seafire F.45 prototype. Contract No. B981687/39 dated March 1942 modified from Spitfire Mk.Vc and later F.21 contracts. Further contract AIR/4424/c.23(c) was issued on 12 December 1945 for production aircraft. Designed to Naval requirement N.7/44. A total of 50 airframes were built.

20 February 1945
Maiden flight of prototype PR.19 also known as the Supermarine Type 389/390. The original contract was dated 2 June 1943. A final total of 225 Spitfire PR.19s were manufactured.

21 March 1945
First flight of Spitfire F.22 built to contract B981687/39 dated 2 June 1943. This contract was originally for Mk.Vc before being changed to the Type 356. The manufacturers constructed a total of 278 of this variant.

2 April 1945
Contract AIR 1877/C.23(c), dated 14 August 1943, converted from the original Spitfire F.21 order to cover the Type 371/393 Spiteful fighter which first flew on this date.

May 1945
No. 802 Sqdn, FAA receives the production Seafire F.XV.

19 June 1945
The first production version of the Spitfire F.XVIII undertakes its maiden flight. These aircraft were originally ordered as Mk.VIII airframes to contract Air/1877/c.23(c) dated 1 December 1942. A total of 300 were constructed.

September 1945
Supermarine Seafire F.XVII enters service with No 88 Sqdn of the Fleet Air Arm.

5 November 1945
First flight of Type 388/374 Seafire F.46 produced to contract B981687/39 originally for Spitfire Mk.Vc dated March 1942. A total of 24 of this version were built.

15 January 1946
Maiden flight of Supermarine Type 396 designated Seafang Mk.31.

27 February 1946
Development of F.22, the F.24, makes its maiden flight. Built to modified contract A/C5795/C.23(c), dated 15 November 1945, it originally covered an order for the F.22. Only 54 of this version were built from new whilst a further 27 were converted from unused F.22 airframes.

25 April 1946
First flight of Seafire F.47, the final version of the type. A final total of 90 airframes were constructed by Supermarine.

September 1946
No. 778 Sqdn (a training unit) re-equips with the Seafire F.45.

August 1947
No. 1832 Sqdn equips with Seafire F.46, the only unit to do so.

April 1949
No. 800 Sqdn FAA re-equips with the Seafire FR.47.

14 June 1957
Final flight by operational Spitfire when THUM Flight retired the remaining Spitfire PR.19s.

Spiteful RB518 was originally built as an F.XIV before being converted to F.XVI standard in 1947. Used mainly as a test aircraft, it suffered a series of engine out landings whilst trialing the Griffon 101 engine and associated contra-rotating propeller assembly. It was finally written off when it made a forced landing after engine failure which pushed the main gear units up through the wings. (C P Russell Smith Collection)